The People Behind Murderous CRIME SPREES

John A. Torres

E | **Enslow Publishing**
101 W. 23rd Street
Suite 240
New York, NY 10011
USA

enslow.com

Published in 2017 by Enslow Publishing, LLC.
101 W. 23rd Street, Suite 240, New York, NY 10011

Copyright © 2017 by Enslow Publishing, LLC.

Library of Congress Cataloging-in-Publication Data
Names: Torres, John Albert, author.
Title: The people behind murderous crime sprees / John A. Torres.
Description: New York, NY : Enslow Publishing, 2017. | Series: The psychology
  of mass murderers | Includes bibliographical references and index.
Identifiers: LCCN 2016001576 | ISBN 9780766076129 (library bound)
Subjects: LCSH: Mass murderers—Juvenile literature. | Criminal
  behavior—Juvenile literature.
Classification: LCC HV6515 .T667 2017 | DDC 364.152/34—dc23
LC record available at http://lccn.loc.gov/2016001576

Printed in the United States of America

To Our Readers: We have done our best to make sure all website addresses in this book were active and appropriate when we went to press. However, the author and the publisher have no control over and assume no liability for the material available on those websites or on any websites they may link to. Any comments or suggestions can be sent by e-mail to customerservice@enslow.com.

Photo Credits: Cover, p. 1 Corepics VOF/Shutterstock.com; throughout book, chrupka/ Shutterstock.com (scratched black background); Merkushev Vasiliy/Shutterstock.com (red background), Tiberiu Stan/Shutterstock.com (brain waves); p. 7 Katherine Welles/ Shutterstock.com; p. 11 Yiorgos GR/Shutterstock.com; p. 13 (top) Mark Wilson/Getty Images, (bottom) Lawrence Jackson-Pool/Getty Images; p. 17 Hulton Archive/Getty Images; p. 21 Al Fenn/The LIFE Picture Collection/Getty Images; p. 23 Carl Iwasaki/The LIFE Images Collection/Getty Images; pp. 27, 38, 48, 58, 93, 96, 114 © AP Images; p. 31 Steve Northup/The LIFE Images Collection/Getty Images; p. 32 Alex Wong/Getty Images; p. 36 vitstudio/Shutterstock.com; p. 42 author unknown/Wikimedia Commons/MutsuoToi. jpg/public domain; p. 46 Art Shay/The LIFE Images Collection/Getty Images; p. 51 H/O/ AFP/Getty Images; p. 52 ROBERT SULLIVAN/AFP/Getty Images; p. 54 Smit/Shutterstock. com; p. 62 Zholobov Vadim/Shutterstock.com; p. 65 Leisa Tyler/LightRocket via Getty Images; p. 66 Fairfax Media/Fairfax Media via getty images; p. 69 KIM JAE-HWAN/AFP/ Getty Images; p 71 akarapong/Shutterstock.com; p. 73 Henry County Police/Liaison/ Getty Images; p. 74 STEVE SCHAEFER/AFP/Getty Images; p 77, Anthony Neste/The LIFE Images Collection/Getty Images; p. 79 AFP/Getty Images; p. 82 Nick Sorrentino/NY Daily News Archive via Getty Images; p. 86 courtesy Everett Collection; p. 89 STEVEN PURCELL/ AFP/Getty Images; p. 92 FABRIZIO VILLA/AFP/Getty Images; p. 99 Photographee.eu/ Shutterstock.com; p. 103 Andybremner2012/Wikimedia Commons/Welcome sign.jpg/ Creative Commons Attribution-Share Alike 3.0 Unported; p. 106 ruigsantos/Shutterstock. com; p. 111 YURI CORTEZ/AFP/Getty Images.

Contents

Traits of a Mass Murderer[1]

1. *Seeks revenge.* In 30 percent of mass killings, family members are the main victims. The next most likely target is the workplace, to take revenge on a boss or coworkers. Some mass murderers blame society and open fire in public places, or they target police.

2. *Has access to high-powered weapons.* Daniel Nagin, a criminologist at Carnegie Mellon University, says, "It's technologically impossible to kill a lot of people very quickly without access to assault weapons."

3. *Blames other people for his or her problems.*

4. *Often has a mental illness, particularly paranoid schizophrenia.*

5. *Is a loner, with few friends or social connections.*

6. *Carefully plans the attacks, taking days to months to get ready.*

7. *Has suicidal tendencies.*

8. *Has made violent threats, to the target or others indirectly, prior to the attack.*

9. *Is often reacting to a stressor just prior to the rampage, such as the loss of a job or a relationship.*

10. *The actions are not often a surprise to those who know him or her.*

INTRODUCTION

What Drives a Person to Kill?

The answers to this question, or at least the theories, are one of the major tools used by law enforcement agencies to apprehend and perhaps prevent these crimes from happening. But as is too often the case, agents trained in profiling killers, or psychologists working with police, are left to analyze crime scenes and murderers only after they have committed atrocious crimes.

How Do You Stop Them? How Do You Save Lives?

Many times, other than monitoring someone who has posted something on social media or told friends about their intentions, the answer is simply to study them. Analyze the crime. Try to find the motivation. Look for similarities and figure out what drives a person to go on a murderous crime spree.

Investigators can often learn much about a killer's personality from the particular crime scenes. And a special branch of the Federal

Bureau of Investigation (FBI) known as the Investigative Services Unit has studied killers and violent offenders in prison in order to develop and identify certain characteristics or traits killers share.

From bank-robbing duos like the notorious Bonnie and Clyde to the seemingly normal law-abiding citizens like Florida's William Cruse, there is little that gains the public's attention and dominates headlines like a murderous crime spree. The questions that always move to the forefront are: Were these crimes preventable? What was the killer's motivation? What exactly was the killer thinking? And is there a cure?

Not all murderous sprees are alike. In fact, law enforcement agencies don't always agree on what exactly defines a spree killer and what differentiates him from a serial killer or a mass murderer. The FBI typically defines a spree killer as someone who kills in more than one location without a cooling off period. They say that a cooling off period would define the person as a serial killer. The FBI also defines a spree killer as having killed in at least three different locations and at three distinct times. Most law enforcement agencies, however, do not buy into the cooling off period as being what determines the labeling of a spree killer or serial killer. They do not feel that serial killers are "cooling off" but rather commit clearly separate murders. As serial killers fulfill their need to kill, oftentimes the murders occur more frequently.

Some experts say that spree killers act out over the course of several weeks and may even use different methods of killing their victims. There may also be different motives, such as the need to eliminate witnesses, killing to ensure a getaway, or the need to kill for killing's sake.

Agents from the FBI collect evidence from a crime scene. The crime scene can yield clues about a killer's personality.

But even the experts don't often agree on how to categorize a killer. For example, Charles Starkweather—a teenager who murdered eleven people in Wyoming and Nebraska over two months in 1957 and 1958—is considered by many to be a spree killer. But he does not fit neatly into the FBI's definition. They would consider him a serial killer because of the length of time between murders. Others have classified him as a mass murderer.

Psychology Today magazine agrees with the FBI's definition of spree killer with one major difference. Experts there suggest that spree killers simply do not resume their normal lives, as a serial killer would after killing someone. They also put the length of time between killings at no more than seven days. By contrast, serial killers can take months and sometimes even years between killings. The Washington DC-area "Beltway Killings" in 2002, where a duo systematically killed ten people in three states over the course of twenty-three days, would not qualify as serial killings under the FBI's definition.

While not all spree killings have a clear motive, *Psychology Today* argues that more often than not spree killers are set off by some emotional and very personal event such as losing a job or a relationship problem. On the contrary, serial killers normally have no emotional connection with their victims or an emotional reason for killing other than fulfilling a deep-seated fantasy.

To confuse matters further, some experts and law enforcement agencies have coined a new phrase that groups both spree killers and mass murderers into one grouping called "rampage killers." The anger, rampage, or emotion is essentially the main difference between rampage killers and serial killers. In any event, a police academy manual states that spree killings and mass murders are on the rise in the United States, and people want to know why.

Politics and gun laws aside, most agree that personality characteristics—whether inherited or formed—are the key to understanding these killers. Most law enforcement agents, homicide detectives, and criminal profilers can define some of the personal attributes exhibited by those who commit heinous crimes. These specific personality traits are an important part of any profile and are often based on crime scene evidence.[2]

The following chapters separate spree killers into groups and attempt to identify similarities and patterns. The definitions may differ as to what exactly constitutes a spree killer, but most everyone agrees on one thing: the killer wants his existence or actions to end and will continue until killed by police or captured and locked away for life.[3] Spree killers do not expect to get away with murder.

Chapter 1

DUOS

Typically, murder sprees are done by single individuals and not by pairs, duos, or groups. But what about the duo or couple working together to commit crimes, who suddenly loses any regard for human life? This chapter will take a look at both types: those who went out with the intention of killing and those who started and could not stop, like bank robbers Bonnie and Clyde.

Not included will be duos who performed heinous murders, like Lyle and Erik Menendez, because they were not spree killers. These brothers murdered their parents in cold blood and then started spending their parents' fortune to support their lavish lifestyles.

Also not included are the notorious Columbine killers—Eric Harris and Dylan Klebold. On April 20, 1999, they went to their Colorado school, Columbine High School, and opened fire on their classmates, killing thirteen and wounding nearly a dozen before shooting themselves. Because of the one shooting event and one location, Klebold and Harris are more mass murderers than spree killers. Also excluded are the murderous crime sprees committed in the somewhat lawless period of the "Wild West". However, the post-American Civil War cold-blooded killers Jesse James and his brother Frank are included, along with the rest of their gang.

From research on murderous duos, it became overwhelmingly clear that for the majority of the time, the pair featured a strong-willed leader and the submissive follower, who might have been trying to simply please the other person.

We often tend to believe that those who commit murder, mass murder, spree killings, or any other heinous, violent acts must be irrational. But that is not the case. More often than not there is a rationality to the killer's thinking. Serial killers, for example, take great care and often a lot of time in choosing their next victim. While the following rationales for killing would likely never drive the majority of us to pick up a gun and murder someone, to the killer it is enough.

Control: The violent person may want to control their victim's behavior or life.

Retribution: The perpetrator may want to punish someone without calling the police or using the justice system to address their grievances. They take the law into their own hands.

Deterrence: The attacker may want to stop someone from repeating acts that they consider hostile or provocative.

Reputation: An attack may be motivated by the need to enhance reputation and create self-importance in the eyes of others.[1]

Crime spree duos are often composed of one leader and a weaker follower, who aims to please the leader.

Psychologists have long struggled to explain how one person can convince another to forget about love, decency, and morality, and to share in their murderous intentions. Does it take two likeminded individuals to come together? What is the secret to convincing a partner to cover up dastardly deeds or even to participate in the murders themselves?

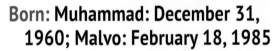
> **Born:** Muhammad: December 31, 1960; Malvo: February 18, 1985
>
> **Occupation:** Muhammad: Retired from US Army; Malvo, high school student
>
> **Arrested:** October 24, 2002
>
> **Died:** Muhammad was executed on November 10, 2009; Malvo is serving a life sentence in prison.

Less than a year after the September 11, 2001, terrorist attacks that toppled the World Trade Center, destroyed part of the Pentagon, and killed more than three thousand people, the country was once again put on alert by random killings along the Washington DC beltway.

The killers—forty-one-year-old John Allen Muhammad and his seventeen-year-old protégé, Lee Boyd Malvo—had started their reign of terror months earlier and thousands of miles away when they pretended to be father and son in the state of Washington.

Muhammad, born John Allen Williams in Baton Rouge, Louisiana, joined the Nation of Islam in 1987 and changed his name one month after the terrorist attacks. He was raised mainly by his grandmother

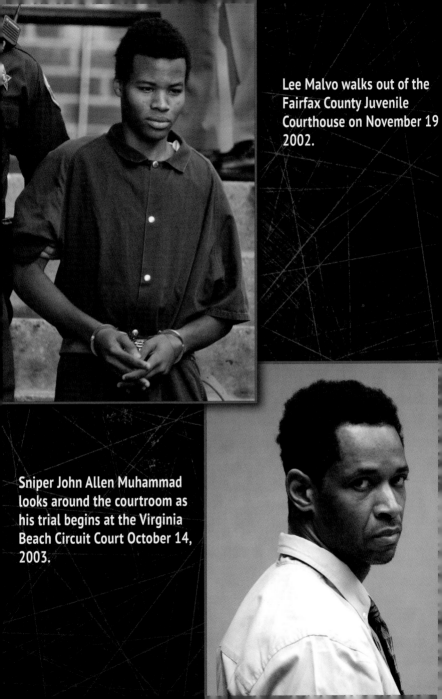

Lee Malvo walks out of the Fairfax County Juvenile Courthouse on November 19 2002.

Sniper John Allen Muhammad looks around the courtroom as his trial begins at the Virginia Beach Circuit Court October 14, 2003.

and aunt in New Orleans after his mother died of cancer when he was only three. He spent nearly twenty years in the US Army, where he served a number of duties and was honorably discharged. But he failed at several business attempts after the army, including an auto repair shop and a karate school. He was starting to become disgruntled.

After two failed marriages, Muhammad kidnapped his own children and fled to the Caribbean island of Antigua, where he became involved in a relationship with Malvo's mother. In Antigua, Muhammad supported himself by engaging in criminal activities such as credit card and immigration fraud.

Malvo and his mother entered the United States illegally through Florida and settled in Bellingham, Washington. Muhammad followed. Malvo's mother was apprehended, so Malvo lived with Muhammad at a shelter, where he pretended to be Muhammad's son.

Police found Muhammad and returned his three children to their mother. Police believe this may have been the trigger that led him on his murderous rampage. A friend of his ex-wife's was murdered near Bellingham, Washington. A month later, in May 2002, a man was shot dead on an Arizona golf course. More shootings and murders followed as Muhammad and Malvo made their way across the country. Ballistic evidence and eyewitness accounts tied the pair to several shootings before they ever started their sniper attacks in the DC area, where Muhammad's ex-wife lived.

Muhammad convinced Malvo that they would hold the nation's capital hostage and force them to pay a large sum of money—$10 million—in order to start a new society in Canada.

Muhammad used his experience as a mechanic to create a sniper's nest in the trunk of a car. The pair would drive around and target random people doing everyday things, such as pumping gas or going shopping. When it was all over, the pair had killed ten and injured three in the DC area.

One of these injured persons called a tip line and a priest to let them know of a clue left behind at an Alabama liquor store shooting—a fingerprint—that ultimately led police to arresting the pair. Malvo testified against Muhammad in court and was himself sentenced to life in prison. Muhammad was sentenced to death and was executed by lethal injection in 2009.

Psychological red flags:

Muhammad became increasingly paranoid and narcissistic over the years. Malvo was vulnerable without a father figure and was easily influenced by the elder man.

Pattern of crime:

Mainly a sniper's rifle

Number of victims:

At least ten as the other two were never proven

aka Bonnie and Clyde

> **Born: Parker: October 1, 1910;**
> **Barrow: March 24, 1909**
>
> **Occupation: Parker: waitress;**
> **Barrow: career criminal**
>
> **Died: Killed by police on May 23,**
> **1934**

There is little doubt that the criminal duo of Bonnie and Clyde are the most well known of the murderous spree killers. That is mainly due to how much the pair were romanticized in movies, songs, and stories well after police shot them dead in 1934. Adding to their almost legendary place in history was the country's fascination with high-profile criminals, especially during the Great Depression. The country's economy was in shambles, people were suffering, and there appeared to be no end in sight.

The country became fascinated with glamorous high-profile gangsters like John Dillinger and "Pretty Boy" Floyd, who seemed fearless as they robbed banks in broad daylight and survived shootouts with police. Bonnie and Clyde took it a step further. They were young, beautiful, and very much in love. And so, it seemed, was America.

The couple, like many others who turned to a life of crime, had a pretty rough start to life. Parker's father died when she was very young. She grew up poor, as she was raised by her single mom, who worked as a seamstress. Most women did not go on to college

Clyde Barrow and Bonnie Parker were known as Bonnie and Clyde. This photo of the American bank robbers and lovers was taken around 1933.

after high school in those days, and so it wasn't surprising when Parker quit high school a week before turning sixteen and married her boyfriend, Roy Thompson. The marriage didn't work out, as Thompson spent more time in jail than with his new bride.

It would be a few years until Parker would meet Clyde Barrow, who grew up in a farming family that lost everything due to the Depression. They were dirt poor and even spent some time living under their wagon because they could not afford a tent. Barrow turned to a life of crime from an early age, committing thefts and burglaries. He was in and out of jail for a variety of offenses when he first laid eyes on Parker at a friend's home.

It was love at first sight.

But Barrow found himself in prison just a short time later. He committed his first murder behind bars, attacking the man who had sexually assaulted him in prison. Barrow killed him with a lead pipe. He then escaped from prison using a gun that Parker smuggled in to him during a visit.

He was caught, sent back to prison, and remarkably given parole after serving only two years. This is when he and Parker embarked on their life of crime. Joined by Barrow's brother and his wife as well as a friend, the five started moving across the country committing outlandish, bold robberies along the way.

Their plan—or rationale—was to steal enough money in order to fund a jailbreak for some friends who were serving long sentences in prison. They were not about to let anything or anyone stand in their way. On April 30, 1932, they pulled a robbery in Hillsboro, Texas, and the store owner was shot and killed.

A few months later, Barrow and his friends shot and killed a deputy and wounded a sheriff who were coming toward Barrow in the parking lot of a country dance, where he was drinking alcohol. It was the first time they shot and killed a law enforcement officer. When their crime spree was over, they had killed nine officers of the law and were accused of killing three civilians, bringing the total to twelve.

After a well-publicized nationwide manhunt that captivated the nation, police ambushed the pair in Louisiana on May 23, 1934. The lawmen hid in the bushes and unloaded 130 bullets into their car, killing Bonnie and Clyde and finally putting an end to their murderous deeds.

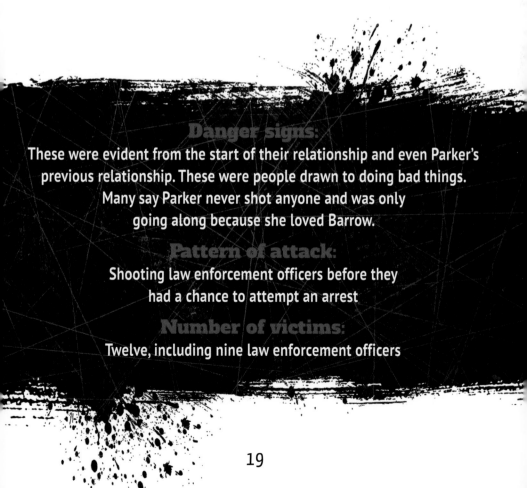

Danger signs:
These were evident from the start of their relationship and even Parker's previous relationship. These were people drawn to doing bad things. Many say Parker never shot anyone and was only going along because she loved Barrow.

Pattern of attack:
Shooting law enforcement officers before they had a chance to attempt an arrest

Number of victims:
Twelve, including nine law enforcement officers

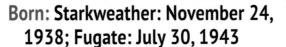

Born: Starkweather: November 24, 1938; Fugate: July 30, 1943

Occupation: Starkweather: warehouse worker; Fugate: student

Died: Starkweather was executed in prison on June 25, 1959; Fugate spent seventeen years in prison and was paroled in 1976.

Like Bonnie and Clyde's, Charles Starkweather and Caril Ann Fugate's sordid tale has served as the inspiration for several movies and even some contemporary music. But the tone was much different. The Starkweather murder spree took place after notorious gangsters of the roaring twenties and early 1930s were looked at as folk heroes. Americans did not glamorize crime in the 1950s, and the duo were looked upon as cold-blooded killers.

Over time, there has been some speculation regarding how much alienation and bullying Starkweather endured, which fueled his rage as a child. Childhood teasing and bullying went virtually unchecked in those days, and Starkweather suffered from misshapen legs due to a childhood condition as well as a speech impediment. The children treated him cruelly, and there was little he could do but bottle up the rage. That is, until he became a teenager and excelled in athletics.[2]

Teenage murderer Charles Starkweather walks into the state penitentiary.

It was in the school's gymnasium and athletic fields that Stark-weather turned the tables on the children who had once bullied him. People who knew him would later say that something drastic changed in him. He went from a pleasant, well-behaved gentleman to a brooding, moody troublemaker.

He started dressing and acting even more differently after seeing James Dean in the movie *Rebel Without a Cause.* It was during this time that he met Fugate, when she was only thirteen years old. He became smitten and quit high school to work at a warehouse near her school so he could see her every day. Fugate's parents were not happy with her relationship with a boy who was nearly five years her senior. They tried to keep the couple apart as best they could.

After crashing his father's car, Starkweather was banished from his home. He then quit the job at the warehouse to become a sanitation worker. His anger grew. In November 1957, roughly two months before the couple embarked on their murderous spree, Starkweather went to a service station on his way to see Fugate. There was a stuffed animal he wanted to get her, but he didn't have the money. He killed the attendant who wouldn't let him have the present on credit. He admitted to Fugate that he robbed the man but denied killing him.

That January, Starkweather went to Fugate's home, but she was not there. Her mother and stepfather told him to stay away from her. Enraged, he killed them both with a shotgun and then even strangled their two-year-old daughter.

When Fugate came home, she helped him hide the bodies on the family property and stayed in the house for several days, until people came looking for her family.

Caril Ann Fugate (left), the girlfriend of teenage murderer Charles Starkweather, sits in jail in 1958.

They went to the home of a family friend and killed the seventy-year-old man with a shotgun blast. They went on a two-state rampage, killing nearly every day they were on the run, even killing two high schoolers in a car and stealing their four dollars.

Three murders happened at the home of one of Lincoln, Nebraska's wealthiest men, C. Lauer Ward. They killed his wife, maid, and dog before waiting for Ward to return home from work; they killed him too.

Starkweather was adamant that Fugate took part in the killings, both shooting and stabbing some of their victims. They were eventually captured by authorities in Wyoming, where Fugate ran to officers claiming that Starkweather forced her to go along or he would kill her.

A judge did not buy her story, noting the multiple opportunities she had to escape, and sentenced her to life in prison. Starkweather was sentenced to death and was executed on June 25, 1959.

Fugate was released after seventeen years.

Danger signs:

Bully victim turned into bully. Starkweather quit school, was a loner, and had an inappropriate relationship with a young girl.

Pattern of attack:

No real pattern. They just killed whoever got in their way.

Number of victims:

Eleven total, though only ten were killed by the duo

Alton Coleman and Debra Brown

> **Born:** **Coleman: November 6, 1955; Brown: November 11, 1962**
>
> **Occupation:** **Coleman: career criminal and rapist; Brown: unemployed.**
>
> **Diagnosis:** **Coleman was described as a sexual deviant and self-loathing African American; Brown has been described as intellectually disabled.**
>
> **Arrested:** **July 20, 1984**
>
> **Died:** **Coleman was executed in prison on April 26, 2002.**

Alton Coleman was already well known to police when he started his murderous crime spree with Debra Brown in 1983. In fact, he was supposed to stand trial for raping a fourteen-year-old girl when the rampage began.

Coleman suffered from several mental health issues, including personality disorder. As a child, he was teased and bullied repeatedly because he often wet his pants. The children nicknamed him Pissy. He was raised by his elderly grandmother in Illinois because his mother was a prostitute. Sometimes she would have sex with her clients in front of him when he was young. Coleman, who dropped out while still in middle school, developed a strong desire for sex and deviant behavior. As he got older, he started forcing himself on women and children. He was charged with multiple sex crimes as a young man. Several charges were dropped and twice he pleaded guilty to lesser charges. He was even charged with raping his young niece.

Coleman should have been sentenced to prison for a long time before he ever started killing. But he had a knack for evading serious jail time. He would sometimes intimidate his victims into changing their story or into dropping charges. Police also said he was very good at conning a jury. He seemed gentle and sincere, as he would claim the police nabbed the wrong man. He credited his belief in and practice of voodoo with protecting him from the law.[3]

In 1983, Coleman's sister went to authorities and told them her brother tried to rape her eight-year-old daughter. Three weeks later, she went to court to have the charges dropped. "It's a misunderstanding," she said. "A lot of families go through that. It doesn't make any difference now."[4]

Debra Brown was one of eleven children in her family and she suffered a severe head trauma as a little girl. She has been diagnosed as being borderline intellectually disabled. She also has been described as having a dependent personality, meaning she was susceptible to manipulation by others she depended upon.

She was engaged to marry another man when she first met Coleman, who convinced her to leave her future husband and move in with him. Her relationship with Coleman has been described as master and slave.

According to several profiles of the killers, Coleman was said to be a self-loathing African American who professed a deep hatred for black people. There is also speculation he may have hated himself because of homosexual tendencies, which added to his rage.

Alton Coleman and Debra Brown appear in court in Cincinnati, Ohio, on January 31, 1985.

It was not long after that the couple committed their first murder: the rape and killing of a nine-year-old girl who was the daughter of their friend in Kenosha, Wisconsin. A few days later they targeted sisters, nine-year-old and seven-year-old girls in Gary, Indiana. Both Coleman and Brown participated in raping and torturing both girls. The older girl escaped but they killed the younger sister.

The killings, rapes, and robberies continued. Their strategy was to befriend their victims, earn their trust, and then kill them. By mid-July 1983, the duo was being hunted by the FBI, who arrested them in Illinois. When their spree was all said and done, they had murdered eight people. With murders across multiple states, the FBI had to figure out where to hold the trial. They chose Ohio because it offered the death penalty.

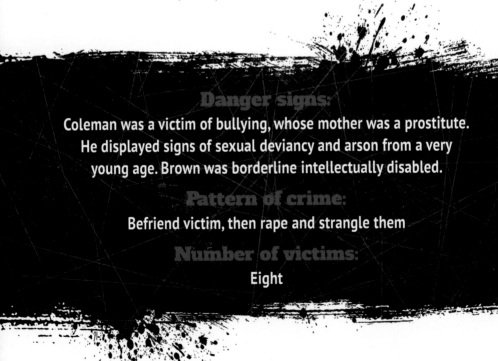

Danger signs:

Coleman was a victim of bullying, whose mother was a prostitute. He displayed signs of sexual deviancy and arson from a very young age. Brown was borderline intellectually disabled.

Pattern of crime:

Befriend victim, then rape and strangle them

Number of victims:

Eight

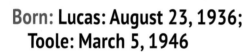

**Born: Lucas: August 23, 1936;
Toole: March 5, 1946**

**Occupation: Lucas: drifter; Toole:
drifter and prostitute.**

Diagnosis: **Lucas may have inherited
mental illness, and was an alcoholic
and victim of sexual abuse as a
child; Toole was diagnosed with a
mild intellectual disability. He was
sexually aroused by setting fires.**

Died: **Lucas: March 12, 2001;
Toole: 1996**

The murderous duo of Henry Lucas and Ottis Toole is classified by some as being serial killers, but the callousness and randomness of choosing their victims can also classify them as spree killers. The two, like many of the others in this book, suffered horrendous childhoods.

Toole, who was born and raised in Jacksonville, Florida, was forced to dress as a girl from a young age, and his mother called him by girls' names. His mother apparently was a Satanist and he was subjected to disturbing images and experiences, like being forced to have sex with his father's friend when he was only five. Toole also claimed to have been the victim of incest at the hands of numerous relatives.

Toole dropped out of school in the sixth grade and had numerous conditions such as epilepsy, dyslexia, and attention deficit hyperactivity disorder (ADHD). He announced he was gay at the age of ten. Toole claimed his first murder victim when he was only fourteen, running down a traveling salesman who had propositioned him for sex. He left home and supported himself by panhandling and prostitution. He was suspected of several murders—in Nebraska and Colorado—before ever even meeting Henry Lee Lucas at a Florida soup kitchen.

Lucas was born in Blacksburg, Virginia, and had a childhood comparable to that of Toole. He lost an eye at a young age when his own brother stabbed him. He was also subjected to bullying and torture because his mother dressed him like a girl. His mother was a prostitute who would service clients in front of her son. His father was found frozen to death outside the family home after passing out drunk.

Like Toole, Lucas dropped out of school in the sixth grade and is reported to have committed his first murder as a young teenager, when he strangled seventeen-year-old Laura Burnsley when she wouldn't have sex with him. Lucas would later recant the confession, a pattern he developed for the rest of his life—confess to horrible crimes and then recant—providing more evidence of his deep psychological issues.

Lucas was sentenced to prison in Michigan, but a psychologist testified that he had made terrific progress, and he was released after only a few years due to overcrowding. While in prison, Lucas studied the methods of famous killers and how to evade police.

Lucas, who killed his own mother after getting released, and Toole became lovers in 1976 and set out across the southeast on

Henry Lucas, pictured here in 1986, died in prison in 2001.

Adam Walsh's father, John Walsh, was the host of the TV show *America's Most Wanted* and cofounder of the National Center for Missing & Exploited Children (NCMEC). Adam Walsh was murdered by Ottis Toole.

a murderous spree that included between eleven and one hundred victims. They claimed that they targeted whomever they met, often drifters like themselves.

The pair became notorious for confessing to murders in exchange for better conditions in prison. The most high profile of their supposed killings, however, was that of Adam Walsh, a six-year-old boy who disappeared from a Miami-area department store, never to be found again. The boy's father, John Walsh, has made it his life's work to help save missing and exploited children. Toole was found to be responsible for the murder after he died, even though he had told police earlier that he decapitated the boy and drove around with his head in the trunk of the car. Psychologists testified at Toole's trials that he suffered from severe paranoid schizophrenia, and for that reason he was sentenced to life in prison instead of getting the death penalty.

Lucas confessed to killing more than 3,000 people after claiming the number was about 100 for years. He was convicted of killing 11 and died in prison. Toole was convicted of murdering 6 people. He also died in prison.

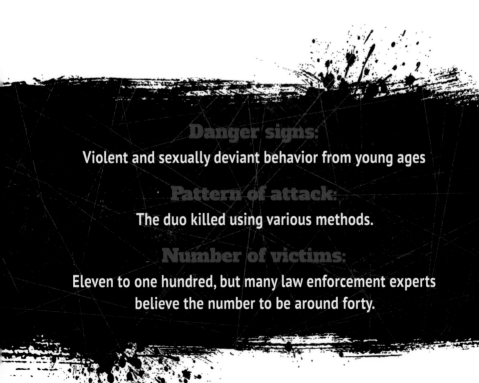

Danger signs:

Violent and sexually deviant behavior from young ages

Pattern of attack:

The duo killed using various methods.

Number of victims:

Eleven to one hundred, but many law enforcement experts believe the number to be around forty.

Chapter 2

Solo
KILLERS

There are many reasons why people turn away from the societal norm to take on a life of crime; even more so is what drives people to murder alone. Most experts agree that the major indicators that determine whether a person will take on antisocial behavior has to do with having challenging upbringings: high-crime environment, poverty, broken home, abusive parents, and drug and alcohol abuse.

That theory would be supported by Sigmund Freud, who was the founder of psychoanalytical theory. He believed that the origins of all abnormal or dangerous behavior were found only in one place: the first five years of a person's life. That would certainly explain a lot of the behaviors exhibited by Henry Lee Lucas and Ottis Toole, who had horrific childhood experiences.

Freud said that the memories often occurred so early in a person's life did not exist as memories but were subconsciously locked away in a person's brain, ready to spring back to the forefront at a moment's notice. But, Freud theorized, we are also equipped with tools to keep these bad memories, experiences, and urges at bay. They are called defense mechanisms and include things like denial, repression, and rationalization. That is why not everyone who has a violent childhood becomes a killer. Defense mechanisms keep unwanted thoughts and feelings from reaching conscious awareness.[1]

But there are some experts, known as constitutional criminologists, who say that some of the reasons for the murderous behavior can be found in the genes. While very few theorists at present now believe that heredity is the sole cause of criminality, constitutional criminological theories still stand.[2]

The constitutional theorists point to studies involving biological twins separated at birth and raised in different homes and environments. The twins went on to exhibit similar criminal and violent behaviors.

The answer is likely a combination of genetics and the environment. Many criminal psychologists hold to the genetic theory but then point to childhood, environment, and other outside forces that act as a trigger for the violent behavior to emerge.

Of course, there are those who simply murder for their own gain, such as Bonnie and Clyde. There is also the school of thought that spree murderers or even certain rampage murderers should be considered serial killers, even if they sought personal gain by killing.

"Our position is that the number of victims, the motivation and the anticipated gain (material or psychological) are all integral to

Some constitutional criminalists believe that the tendency for murderous behavior may be partially dictated by a person's genes, which are located in one's DNA.

the definition of a serial killer. In other words, we believe that one can kill serially for money or for sex and still be determined a serial killer," wrote criminologists Ronald and Stephen Holmes.[3]

Whatever the reason, the following profiles involve spree killers who acted alone for the most part and who were driven to kill by a variety of different reasons.

aka Pretty Boy Floyd

Born: February 3, 1904

Occupations: Bank robber, career criminal

Died: October 22, 1934

Charles Arthur Floyd was born in Georgia in 1904. But his family moved to Oklahoma to become farmers when he was still very young. The family was poor and struggled to get by. Making matters worse was the onset of the Great Depression and a drought in the Midwest that caused what is known as the "dust bowl." Crops died and many families lost their farms and homes when the crops did not grow.

Unlike many other violent criminals, Floyd's legacy has evoked empathy ,and he is often seen as a tragic figure, one who was driven to his life of crime by the circumstances of his life—mainly the Depression and drought. In fact, legendary American author John Steinbeck mentions Floyd's tragic life more than once in his classic novel about the dust bowl, *The Grapes of Wrath*.

Before he turned to a life of crime and earned the moniker Pretty Boy, Floyd was known to his friends as Choc, because he loved to drink Choctaw Beer—a home-brewed beer first invented by the Choctaw Nation, a tribe of American Indians. The sale of alcohol was illegal during the years of prohibition, so bootleggers would brew and sell it illegally.

Charles "Pretty   n a 1932 photo.

Floyd's first run-in with the law came when he was only eighteen years old. He was caught stealing $3.50 in coins from the US Post Office. A few years later he was arrested for robbing a company's payroll and was sentenced to five years in prison.

He had gotten married before the arrest, and his son was born while he was in jail. He served nearly four years of his sentence and vowed to never go to prison again. But he wasn't going straight either. In fact, he made lots of criminal connections while in prison and started robbing banks and acting as a hired gun, protecting bootleggers when he was released.

Floyd and his wife broke up before he was released.

There are several stories as to how Floyd got his nickname. One is that it was given to him by a girlfriend at a Kansas City boarding-house. Another is that a witness to one of his robberies described him as merely a boy, with pretty apple cheeks. Either way, Floyd apparently hated the name.

He was accused of murdering the man who killed his father but was acquitted. During the late 1920s and early 1930s, Floyd robbed several banks, killed numerous police officers, and even killed rival bootleggers as well. He was known for his violent and careless use of a submachine gun.

Despite the murders, he was seen as a hero by some. During his bank robberies, Floyd would often destroy mortgage documents, which freed homeowners from having to pay their large debts. This even earned him the nickname of Robin Hood of Cookson Hills.

In freeing a friend from the police, Floyd and other criminals took part in the Kansas City Massacre that resulted in four law enforcement officers getting killed. He denied involvement in the massacre until his death.

When gangster John Dillinger was killed, Floyd became Public Enemy No. 1 and was hunted relentlessly. He was finally shot and killed by the FBI in 1934.

Danger signs:

Abject poverty led to anger and crime

Pattern of attack:

Killed witnesses and police during robberies

Number of victims:

Unknown, believed to be between five and twelve

Born: March 5, 1917

Occupation: None

Diagnosis: Tuberculosis, hikimori, hypersexuality

Died: May 31, 1938, by suicide

Mutsuo Toi was born into a well-to-do family in prewar Japan in the city of Tsuyama. He was a smart boy and enjoyed a good childhood with many friends, until both his parents died from tuberculosis. He and his sister then went to live with their grandmother, who raised them.

Things started changing for Toi once he turned seventeen. He became withdrawn and socially awkward. He shut himself in his home and would remain there for months at a time. This condition in Japan is known as "hikimori," and is a phenomenon that affects adolescent males.

The condition has been compared to forms of autism and Asperger's syndrome, and it comes on slowly. Some Japanese mental health experts theorize that it starts with some rejection at school and the realization that the pressures of the outside world and the expectation to succeed is too great. It must be noted that this phenomenon only affects wealthier families, who can afford to have an adult or teenage son remain home. Poorer families need that son to work, thus he is forced into leaving the house and into social situations.

Born in Japan, Mutsuo Toi was a withdrawn young man who was uncomfortable in social situations.

Things became worse for Toi when his sister married and left the family home. This left the hermit-like boy with his grandmother. During this time, there was a notorious case of a Japanese woman who smothered her lover during sex and then mutilated his sexual organs. Her name was Sada Abe. She carried around his sexual organs until her arrest in 1936, shortly after the murder. Toi became fascinated with the story and started to become obsessed with sex and women. He also apparently started writing a sexual novel during this time.

Toi started creeping around the village and sneaking into the windows of single women in the middle of the night, asking for sex. This strange behavior is known in Japan as "nightcrawling," or Yobai. He became addicted to sex, known as hypersexuality, and women began to shun him.

The rejections became worse when Toi himself was diagnosed with tuberculosis, which was both a contagious and fatal disease.

On May 21, 1938, Toi had had enough and wanted revenge for those he claimed had rejected him. Though he loved his grandmother, Toi beheaded her with an axe.

He viewed that as a mercy killing, as he wrote in a suicide note; he did not want her living with the shame of being the grandmother of a murderer. He then tied two flashlights to his head, and armed with a Browning shotgun, an axe, and a katana sword set out to destroy the town.

He cut the electricity cables leading into the town and systematically went from house to house on a murderous rampage. Most people were sleeping when he crept into their homes. The ninety-minute massacre claimed twenty-nine more lives—nearly the entire population of that village. His victims ranged from ages five to eighty-six.

At dawn, Toi aimed the shotgun at his own chest and pulled the trigger, killing himself.

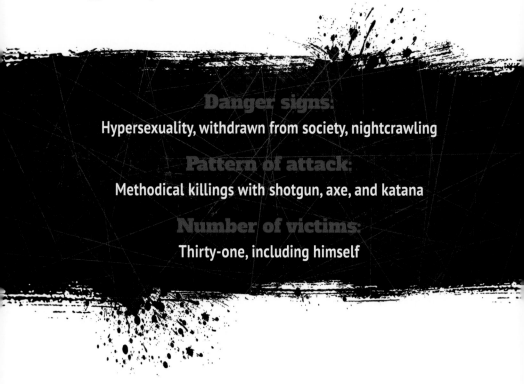

Danger signs:

Hypersexuality, withdrawn from society, nightcrawling

Pattern of attack:

Methodical killings with shotgun, axe, and katana

Number of victims:

Thirty-one, including himself

Born: **December 6, 1941**

Occupations: **Laborer for 7-Up bottling company, ship worker**

Died: **December 5, 1991**

Richard Benjamin Speck's life changed forever the day his father died. Before that, his life was good. He was born in 1941 in Kirkwood, Illinois, into a large, religious family. He was the seventh of eight children in the household.

The happy family suffered a major blow when Speck's father died when the boy was only six. What happened next shaped Speck's future. His mother remarried and moved the family to Texas. Speck's stepfather was a raging alcoholic who was prone to abuse.

Acting out in a rebellious nature, Speck did poorly in school. He had a lifelong fear of people staring at him, and so he refused to read aloud in class or answer any questions. He often failed class because of this and soon became mischievous. That eventually led to drinking alcohol and committing small crimes. He was in and out of juvenile court, as his crimes slowly became more serious.

He married and had a daughter in 1962, but the marriage did not last because he was unable to stay out of trouble. He served time for fraud and aggravated assault. The marriage fell apart in 1966, and Speck's self-control seemed to as well.

He fled from burglary and assault charges to Illinois, where one of his sisters lived. He found work as a carpenter, and then aboard

Richard Speck, pictured here arriving at his trial, was found guilty of murdering

a ship, but dead bodies would be discovered everywhere Speck seemed to go. The barmaid at the tavern he went to every night was brutally raped and killed. Another three girls vanished from Indiana during the time his ship had been there. Four dead women were discovered in Michigan, again, while his ship was in that vicinity in early July.

Police questioned him regarding some of the cases, but he was able to flee every time. His rage continued to grow and by mid-July, he became one of the most infamous killers of all time. On July 13, he forced his way into a house shared by nine nursing students near a Chicago hospital. He rounded up eight of them—while one hid under the bed—and systematically raped and tortured them before strangling, beating, and stabbing them to death.

He stole their money and left. The woman who hid however, was able to tell police about his tattoo, "Born to raise hell," and he was soon identified. Speck slit his wrists in a hotel bathtub, but then he changed his mind about suicide and went to the hospital,where he was arrested.

Speck was originally believed to have XYY Syndrome which is a genetic chromosome abnormality. There were many newspaper accounts written about him and the condition, which later turned out to be false. This is an example of how tough it is for psychologists, criminologists, and other experts to make a definitive diagnosis in these cases.

He was found guilty of killing the eight nurses and sentenced to death. That sentence was later changed to life in prison. Years later, an undercover prison video showed Speck bragging about strangling the nurses. Richard Speck died of a heart attack in 1991.

The People Behind Murderous Crime Sprees

From left, top, are student nurses Gloria Davy, 23, Mary Ann Jordan, 23, Suzanne Farris, 22, and Valentia Pasion, 23, and bottom, Patricia Matusek, 21, Marlita Gargullo, 21, Pamela Wilkening, 22, and Nina Schmale, 21, who were slain in 1978 by Richard Speck.

Danger signs:

Descent into crime, alcoholism

Pattern of attack:

Rape and strangulation

Number of victims:

At least eight confirmed

Born: August 31, 1969

Occupation: Prostitute

Diagnosis: Antisocial personality disorder

Died: July 23, 1997

Born and raised in Southern California, Cunanan was the son of a Filipino-American father and an Italian-American mother. His dad was serving and fighting in the Vietnam War when Cunanan was born.

His mother was religious and his father was a disciplinarian, but Cunanan had a nice childhood. He did not experience any of the childhood traumas and violence that many other spree killers did. He was an exceptional student and was said to have an IQ of 147. Friends remembered him as smart, friendly, and talkative. They did, however, point to one disturbing character trait they did not like— Cunanan's penchant for telling tall tales. He was known as a prolific liar, who would exaggerate greatly and make up fantastic stories about himself and his family.

Cunanan was also known for his ability to greatly change his appearance to stand out, as fashions and hairstyles changed over the years. A big change did occur in his life during his nineteenth year, shortly after he graduated from high school. His father, Modesto Cunanan—who was being investigated for embezzling a large sum of money—abandoned the family to avoid arrest and imprisonment.

Later that year, Cunanan announced to his mother that he was gay. Being a deeply religious woman, she was upset at the news, and they got into a heated argument. Cunanan apparently shoved his mother against the wall so hard that she dislocated her shoulder. Their relationship was never the same after that. He was later thought to have suffered from antisocial personality disorder, which is characterized by not showing any signs of empathy.[4]

Cunanan spent a short time attending college in San Diego before dropping out and moving to San Francisco. He immersed himself in the gay club scene and made money as a prostitute. He started using and selling drugs. He was also obsessed with violent pornography and took part in some snuff films.

He learned to speak several languages and enjoyed living a wealthy-type of lifestyle. But by 1997, the fun times seemingly came to an end. No one is really sure what set Cunanan on his murderous spree. But during this time it is believed that a wealthy lover broke off their relationship. Cunanan may also have believed that he was HIV-positive. HIV is the virus that can lead to AIDS.

Cunanan traveled to Minneapolis and claimed his first victim, former lover Jeffrey Trall. Four days later he killed his second victim, David Madson, who was found shot to death on a lake shore. Police found Trall's body inside Madson's home.

After he killed seventy-two-year-old Lee Miglin in Chicago, the FBI put Cunanan on its Most Wanted list. He killed another man in New Jersey before heading south to Miami Beach, where he openly hung out in the gay clubs and even used his own name.

That July, Cunanan killed his final victim, famous fashion designer and gay icon, Gianni Versace. He eluded police for several days before shooting himself in a Miami houseboat. His motives still remain a mystery, as an autopsy revealed that he was HIV-negative.

FBI FUGITIVE PUBLICITY **TEN MOST WANTED FUGITIVE**

rime Alert: Andrew Phillip Cunanan

WANTED BY THE FBI

ARMED AND EXTREMELY DANGEROUS

Andrew Phillip Cunanan

THE CRIME

Andrew Phillip Cunanan has been charged with the murder of David Madson in Chisago County, Minnesota. Authorities believe that he fled Minnesota in Madson's Jeep Cherokee.

Several days later, authorities discovered the Jeep abandoned, on a street where Chicago, Illinois authorities wen investigating a murder. Discovered missing from this crime scene was the victim's 1994 Lexus, which later turned up in a cemetery parking lot in Pennsville, New Jersey.

In Pennsville, New Jersey, authorities were called to a cemetery when the caretaker failed to return home from work on Friday, 5/9/97. The caretaker was discovered murdered. His vehicle was also reported to be missing. There are strong similarities between this murder and the other murders committed in Minnesota and Illinois.

The caretaker's vehicle is described as a red 1995 Chevy pick-up, with a dark interior, bearing New Jersey license plate KH993D.

REWARD: The FBI is offering $10,000 for information leading to the apprehension of Cunanan.

REMARKS

Andrew Phillip Cunanan

Cunanan may wear prescription eyeglasses. He allegedly has ties to the gay community. He portrays himself as

This picture taken from the FBI website shows Andrew Phillip Cunanan, who murdered Italian fashion designer Gianni Versace.

This houseboat in Miami, Florida was stormed by a SWAT team on reports that Andrew Cunanan was inside. Police discovered his body inside.

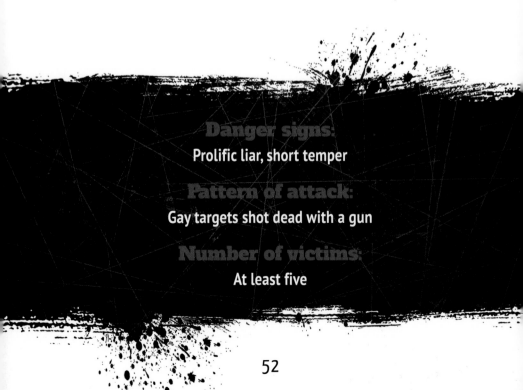

Danger signs:

Prolific liar, short temper

Pattern of attack:

Gay targets shot dead with a gun

Number of victims:

At least five

Chapter 3

Rampage
KILLERS

As discussed earlier, the term "rampage killer" is a fairly new phrase. It encompasses certain elements of being a spree killer and those of mass murderers.

The biggest difference that perhaps sets the rampage killer apart from a traditional spree killer is that the person about to go on the murderous rampage has pretty much given up on society and totally alienated himself from the rest of the world.

While a traditional mass murderer kills in one location, the rampage spree killer will use more than one location, and maybe even incorporate a short cooling off period between murders.

The People Behind Murderous Crime Sprees

Criminologists and authors James Alan Fox and Jack Levin describe four reasons why rampage killings take place. They are:

Revenge killers who seek to get even with individuals or society at large. Their typical target is an estranged wife or employer.

Love killers are motivated by a warped sense of devotion.

Profit killers are usually trying to cover up a crime, eliminate witnesses, or carry out a criminal conspiracy.

Terrorist killers are trying to send a message.[1]

What is typically not counted as or considered mass murders or rampage murders are war crimes or political terrorism. For example, the genocide of millions by Adolph Hitler's Third Reich during World War II is not considered a mass murder or rampage killing.

Rampage killers strike out because of revenge, devotion, profit seeking, or passion.

But again, not every despondent lover or fired employee reaches that breaking point of wanting to commit mass murder, or any violent act for that matter. Josh Buckholtz, a Harvard neuroscientist has worked for years researching and trying to prove whether there are biological roots or causes of violent behavior. "When we compare people who commit violent acts against people who don't commit violent acts, some brain differences begin to emerge: differences in brain circuitry that's involved in emotional arousal and emotion regulation," he said during a television interview, adding that "it is terribly complicated to try and pinpoint one reason why someone becomes violent.

"One of the most infuriating things, as a scientist and as a person, is this attempt to try and find some diagnostic label, some neat diagnostic box to put this person into, and thus explain why they did this terrible, terrible thing," he said.[2]

Most agree that it is a complex combination between nature and nurture that results in the people profiled in this book. This chapter takes a look at mass murderers who killed in more than one location, making them rampage killers under the spree killer heading.

The first killer profiled is a man whom the author has written about extensively and corresponded with professionally while the killer was on Florida's death row. Purposely left out are any school shootings, as they will be profiled in another book dedicated to that classification of murder.

William Bryan Cruse Jr.

Born: **November 21, 1927**

Occupation: **Retired librarian**

Diagnosis: **Delusional paranoia**

Died: **2009 on Florida's death row**

The author of this book was a reporter covering crime and justice for *Florida Today* when he first heard of William Bryan Cruse. He was already an old man when he started writing letters to the author from Florida's death row in Starke to complain about his eyesight, treatment at the hands of the corrections officers, and his overall medical care. It seemed a far cry from the day roughly twenty years earlier when he left his Palm Bay home on a murderous mission.

Cruse was born and raised in Kentucky, where his grandfather owned a farm. His childhood was nondescript, except for having to deal with an alcoholic father who had a bad temper.

When Cruse was young, his father was jailed for shooting into the home of an area prosecutor while he was on a drinking binge. Still, Cruse was intelligent and earned a college degree and then a position as a librarian, a post he held until he retired and moved to Florida.

In his late fifties, Cruse began to display signs of paranoia and anger. He was unhappy that he had to care for his sick wife. He was unhappy that neighborhood kids would take shortcuts through his backyard, and he was sure that everyone was talking about him, especially the baggers at the supermarket.

Cruse was paranoid that people thought he was gay, a fear that followed him from Kentucky to Florida. It wasn't uncommon for him to run out of his home and fire his gun into the air to warn neighbors not to walk in his backyard or not to call him gay. Before his killing spree, he was taken in by police for yelling obscenities at some of the neighboring children. He told police they had yelled gay slurs at him.

By April 23, 1987, he had already had enough. Two kids were bouncing a basketball, and it was driving him mad. He felt that every single bounce was directed at him, taunting him.

Finally, around dinner time, he grabbed three guns and a bag of ammunition and left his home. He shot a fourteen-year-old in the leg, got into his Toyota, and started out for the shopping center nearby.

He stopped at an intersection, where he shot and killed two college students. He drove to a Publix supermarket, where he killed a sixty-seven-year-old woman. When he could not get into the store, he angrily got into his car and drove across the street to the Winn-Dixie supermarket, where he shot and killed two policemen and a bystander.

A shopper grabbed his handgun and engaged Cruse in a short firefight that allowed dozens to flee the supermarket unharmed. He then entered the market and took a hostage for six hours before tear gas canisters fired by police forced him to surrender.

His lawyers tried to get him off using an insanity defense, but a jury convicted him on six counts of murder. He was sentenced to death but was later ruled incompetent on death row. He remained

William Cruse was charged with six counts of first-degree murder. In addition, he injured at least thirteen people at a shopping center in Palm Bay, Florida.

there until 2009, when he died of natural causes at the age of eighty-two.

His hostage felt Cruse should not have been left to die on Florida's death row. "If he wasn't going to be executed, then it's a crying shame that he wasn't found insane and hospitalized for the last twenty years," said Robin Mucha, Cruse's hostage who survived the ordeal.[3]

Danger signs:

Increased paranoia, delusions, and anger

Pattern of attack:

Used several firearms to shoot random people

Number of victims:

Six

Campo Elias Delgado

Born: May 14, 1934

Occupations: Soldier, English teacher

Diagnosis: Possible post-traumatic stress disorder

Died: December 14, 1986, shot by police

Born in Chinacota, Colombia, Campo Elias Delgado witnessed a horrific event as a child, which stayed with him for the rest of his life. He was present when his father committed suicide. Delgado would go on to blame his mother for the suicide and never forgive her for it, saying she had driven his father to do it. Delgado was left with his mother and a sister he never really got along with, claiming she resented him.

Other than that traumatic event, Delgado had a normal upbringing and was a bright student. After attending the university, Delgado moved to Argentina, where he married and had two children. Eventually he moved to the United States, and this is where there are some major discrepancies in the time line of his life.

Many accounts say that Delgado served in the US military and saw extensive action in the Vietnam War. After his shooting spree, however, US government officials said they could not confirm whether Delgado actually served.

Claiming he had seen lots of combat, Delgado returned to his friends, who said he had changed. His marriage failed as did a second one. He was distant and was no good in social situations. He became further and further withdrawn. After getting into an altercation with a thief in New York City, he decided to move back to Colombia, where he lived with his mother. That would turn out to be a big mistake.

The pair never got along. They fought constantly, and sometimes the disagreements even turned violent, according to some accounts. Still, he tried to get on with his life, giving private teaching lessons and taking graduate classes at the university.

No one knows exactly what happened to push the antisocial man over the edge, but on December 3, 1986, Delgado closed out his bank account of nearly $50,000. He purchased a revolver handgun and five hundred rounds of ammunition.

The carnage began the next afternoon, shortly after 2 p.m. He arrived at the apartment of a woman and her fourteen-year-old daughter, to whom he had been giving English lessons. He bound them and stabbed them to death. He returned home and a few hours later, after engaging his mother in a vicious argument, Delgado walked up behind her and stabled her in the neck, killing her. He then set her and their apartment on fire and walked through the apartment complex, yelling "Fire! Fire!" He shot anyone that came out of their apartment, killing numerous neighbors.

He calmly went to a fancy restaurant, Il Pozzetto, and ordered a bottle of wine and a spaghetti dinner. After he was done eating, Delgado ordered several vodka drinks and began reading a magazine. It was 9:15 p.m. when Delgado pulled out his revolver and started opening fire in the crowded restaurant. He targeted certain individuals, chased them down, cornered them, and then shot them in the forehead. The carnage continued until police

With his cash savings, Campo Elias Delgado purchased a revolver to carry out his killings.

arrived ten minutes later and shot Delgado in the head, killing him.

According to some reports, several victims may have been killed accidentally by police, who were using an Uzi-style gun and ammunition. Delgado's story was turned into a well-known book in Colombia and corresponding movie.

Danger signs:

Increasing solitude and resentment

Pattern of attack:

Armed with a handgun and a knife, he targeted people at a popular restaurant.

Number of victims:

Twenty-nine

Martin John Bryant

Born: **May 7, 1967**

Occupation: **On disability due to mental incompetency**

Diagnosis: **Personality disorder, Asperger's syndrome among others**

Family and friends say there was always something different about Martin Bryant, almost from the day he was born in Hobart, Australia. His family, loving and hardworking, noticed that before the child turned one year old, he seemed to reject any attempts at cuddling or affection. Then, as soon as he was able to start crawling, he tried escaping his crib, playpen, or home whenever he could.

His parents started to harness him on the front porch with his toys, so he wouldn't wander off. His energy was almost machinelike,, as he never tired, and his family began to worry when his speech was very slow to develop and his motor skills were clearly impaired.

By the time he was three years old, they were sure there was something seriously wrong with their blond-haired boy. At elementary school, his energy and antics usually irritated his classmates, as he did not know how to communicate normally with them.

Trying to encourage his son to take up a hobby and leave the house once in a while, his father made the terrible mistake of buying him an air rifle one year for his birthday. Bryant became obsessed with firearms. He would often hide in the gully of the road and shoot BBs at oncoming traffic. Another time, he shot a parrot out of a tree, and then proceeded to shoot it several more times to make sure it was dead.

His IQ was so low that some testing during this time concluded that he may have been intellectually disabled. But later, it would be learned that he suffered from conduct disorder, Asperger's syndrome, and attention deficit disorder.

By the time he entered high school, Bryant had become a reclusive loner. He went to a special school, and when he was done he was given a medical pension—the equivalent of social security disability benefits in the United States. In his early twenties, he spent most of his time watching television for the next few years, until he met an eccentric elderly heiress with whom he struck an unlikely friendship.

The platonic relationship started with the woman hiring him to do odds and ends. Eventually he moved in and tended to the older woman, who had dozens of cats and dogs living in the home. Eventually, animal services were called in and discovered Bryant and the woman were living in filth and squalor. The woman was hospitalized and eventually passed away, leaving a huge hole in Bryant's life. He spiraled even further when his father died as well.

The carnage began on April 28, 1996, when Bryant shot and killed a couple, whom he blamed for beating his father to a real estate deal he wanted to do before dying.

Then Bryant went to the Port Arthur ruins, an outdoor museum of prison grounds from the 1800s, and had breakfast in a café. When he was done, he set up a video camera on the table, took a semiautomatic rifle from his bag, and began killing people. Then he walked to the parking lot and starting shooting people as they got in and out of their vehicles. He then flagged down a car, killed

The memorial for the Port Arthur massacre, where Martin Bryant killed thirty-five people, is located at a former British penal station that is now an open-air museum. Following the massacre, strict gun control laws were introduced in Australia.

Emergency services personnel inspect the ruins of the Seascape Guesthouse, where gunman Martin Bryant retreated after shooting and killing thirty-five people during the Port Arthur massacre.

all four occupants, and drove the car away. He stopped later at an intersection and gunned down a mother and her children, leaving the car to chase down one of the children.

Police surrounded the home of Bryant's first victim, where he hid with a hostage the following day. The hostage became Bryant's last victim. Bryant was captured and sentenced to thirty-five life sentences.

Danger signs:

Inept social skills, erratic behavior, unpredictability

Pattern of attack:

Shot victims randomly at popular tourist spot

Number of victims:

Thirty-five

Woo Bum-Kon

aka Power

Born: February 4, 1955

Occupation: South Korean police officer

Diagnosis: Inferiority complex

Died: committed suicide on April 27, 1982

There is very little documentation about the childhood of South Korean Woo Bum-Kon. He was born on February 4, 1955, in Gyeongsangnam-do, a southern province of South Korea. What is known about the man, who was nicknamed Power, is that he had a fierce temper that could be set off by the slightest provocation. He was also prone to violence when he drank alcohol.

If Woo suffered any form of mental illness, then he was able to disguise it well enough to go through years of military training in one of South Korea's toughest military outfits, the marines. After his military tenure, he trained to become a police officer and was hired and stationed by the national police in Busan.

He was later transferred to a local station in the mountainous region of Kungyu, where he lived with his girlfriend. Apparently, their living arrangement was the source of gossip in town, something that upset Woo. Before becoming one of the worst spree killers in history, Woo apparently told friends that he had been feeling depressed and anxious.

Woo Bum-Kon trained for years in South Korea's marines.

The People Behind Murderous Crime Sprees

It all started on the afternoon of April 26, 1982. The twenty-seven-year-old was taking a nap before having to go to work at the police station, when his girlfriend abruptly woke him by swatting a fly that had landed on his chest. Woo was so outraged that she woke him that way that he left the apartment in a huff and reported to work, where he started drinking heavily. A few hours later he returned home in a rage. He beat her and ransacked their apartment, smashing furniture. His girlfriend later told police that he had suffered from an inferiority complex.

He then went back to the police station where, unnoticed, he stole several rifles, grenades, and ammunition. At 9:30 that evening, Woo positioned himself behind some bushes in the town and began firing his rifle and killing people, starting what would become the Uiryeong massacre. When his girlfriend, who heard the shooting, came outside to investigate, he wounded her with a shot in the leg.

He then traveled to a nearby village and shot and killed three operators in the post office. He cut the phone lines so no one could call for help. He went to another nearby village, where he started gaining entry into homes by saying he was there on police business. Woo shot and killed them all.

Many people ran into the nearby rice paddy fields to escape. He killed eighteen people in one village and twenty-four in another. He killed one of the families with a hand grenade.

The police tracked him down at a farmhouse the following morning, where he was hiding with three hostages. Instead of surrendering and releasing the hostages, he blew up a grenade and killed himself and the others.

The final toll was fifty-seven dead and another thirty-five injured.

Many of the people terrorized by Woo Bum-Kon fled to the nearby rice paddies to escape the killer.

Danger signs:

Increasing depression and anger

Pattern of attack:

Used a variety of weapons and stealth to kill victims

Number of victims:

Fifty-seven

71

Born: **April 2, 1955**

Occupation: **Day trader**

Diagnosis: **Driven by financial distress**

Died: **July 29, 1999, suicide as police were closing in on him**

Mark Barton was the only child of parents in the air force. They moved around a little when he was young, and it was tough for him to settle down, grow roots, and make lasting friendships. He was a decent student and earned a degree in chemistry from Clemson University in South Carolina. It was soon after graduating that he met his wife, Debra Spivey.

The couple settled in Texarkana, Texas, where Barton was the president of a chemical company he started with friends. But greed drove him to possibly defraud clients and maybe sell chemicals to people manufacturing illegal drugs. Whatever the reason, he was investigated and eventually fired from his $86,000-a-year job. After sabotaging some of the company's computers, he served a short jail term.

The family moved to Alabama, and in 1993 he became the prime suspect in the murder of his wife and mother-in-law. Barton was having an affair with another woman and had just taken out a large life insurance policy on his wife days before her murder. The police wanted to arrest Barton but did not have enough evidence. He was also suspected of sexually molesting his young daughter

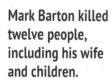

Mark Barton killed twelve people, including his wife and children.

at the time. A psychologist who treated him later said that he was certainly capable of homicide and homicidal thoughts.

Barton wound up marrying the woman he was having an affair with and became a day trader in an Atlanta suburb. But by the spring of 1999, things had started to sour in the relationship. In addition, Barton was losing a ton of money playing high-risk volatile stocks. His wife left him and he started to spiral into despair.

His suicide note read: "I have been dying since October. Wake up at night so afraid, so terrified that I couldn't be that afraid while awake. It has taken its toll. I have come to hate this life and this system of things. I have come to have no hope."[4]

Atlanta residents attend an interfaith memorial service on August 4, 1999, at Peachtree Road United Methodist Church. The service was dedicated to twenty people killed in Atlanta, including those shot by Mark Barton.

On July 27, 1999, he bludgeoned his wife to death with a hammer and hid her body in a closet so his children would not find her. The following day he did the same to them before writing the rambling suicide note saying he would get even with everyone who had tried to bring about his demise.

He then drove to two stock-trading companies he was affiliated with and opened fire, killing four at the first location and five at the second. He got into his van and took a young girl hostage as he tried to escape. Somehow the girl got away and called the police.

Barton killed himself before police could arrest him.

The father of his first wife, William Spivey, blamed the Alabama police for the tragedy, saying that they should have had enough evidence to convict Barton in the murder of his wife and mother-in-law in 1993.

Danger signs:

Became distraught after losing more than $100,000 in stock trades

Pattern of attack:

Targeted two specific stock trading companies

Number of victims:

Twelve

Chapter 4

Gangland

MURDERERS

The American Mafia has been publicized and sometimes glorified over the years in movies like *The Godfather, Goodfellas, Casino*, and *State of Grace*. And of course, who hasn't heard of fictional cable television mobster Tony Soprano?

The crime syndicates—with their origins in Italy—sprouted up in the United States mainly during the American prohibition era, providing illicit alcohol and amassing fortunes. Their attention later turned to drugs, gambling, prostitution, and other rackets. They also controlled legitimate businesses such as waste management, construction, and labor unions.

Originally there was only one major crime family in a major city, except for New York, which was ruled by five families. At one time

Actors Michael Imperioli, James Gandolfini, Tony Siroco, and Steve Van Zandt were cast in the popular HBO TV series *The Sopranos*.

there were about twenty major crime families across the United States, and they even formed a commission or alliance to try to work together to straighten out disputes.

At one time, there was a group of organized contract killers, which was started by Bugsy Siegel and Myer Lansky after they disbanded their own gang. The group carried out thousands of murders for the Mafia. They were backed by their friend Lucky Luciano. Their enterprise became known as Murder Incorporated, and it was as brazen as its moniker might suggest.

There was a certain code among the families, such as never speaking of the criminal activities to anyone outside the family and especially never to law enforcement. Some individual families instituted their own rules as well. For instance, Carlos Gambino threatened to kill anyone in his crime family who was caught dealing drugs. It was simply prohibited.

Over the years, other ethnic groups have taken over some of the criminal enterprises and the murder that goes along with it. There is the Irish mob in Boston and the Russian mob in New York, to name a few. Sometimes they intersected. Members of a deadly and notorious Irish gang in New York known as The Westies were often hired by the Italian Mafia to carry out certain murders for them.

As gangs, or families, fought for greater control and more territory, murder became another tool to go along with intimidation, blackmail, bribery, and extortion when other methods did not accomplish their goals. Sometimes murder was simply part of business, and sometimes it was done to exact revenge over some slight or insult, or to clear the way for someone's rise to power. Of course, the gang leaders who ordered these murders or hits would almost

Al Capone, aka Scarface, appeared during his 1931 trial for federal income tax evasion. America's best-known gangster died from a heart attack at home in 1947, after spending eight years in jail.

never commit the deed themselves, choosing instead to rely on family assassins or contracted killers, known as hitmen.

Some of these bosses did have to commit murder on their way to the top. Some of the more well-known murderous bosses were Al Capone, Lucky Luciano, John Gotti, and Whitey Bulger. Sometimes their hitmen were as well known as they were, like Sammy "The Bull" Gravano and Richard "Iceman" Kuklinski.

This chapter will take a look at some of the hitmen, who did the actual killing, and some of the most murderous bosses, the men who had their fingers on the button and used it the most. Salvatore Riina, nicknamed "The Beast," is believed to have killed forty people and ordered the murders of hundreds of others. Notorious murder sprees with ties primarily to narcotics—such as Joaquin "El Chapo" Guzman—will be featured in another chapter.

While major organized crime was nearly wiped out by the end of the twentieth century, the terrorist attacks of September 11, 2001, brought about a resurgence in mob-related activities. This is due to the fact that the government had to move many of its crime-stopping resources to combat terrorism.

Francis T. Featherstone
aka Mickey Featherstone

> Born: **June 3, 1949**
>
> Occupation: **Enforcer for The Westies gang**
>
> Diagnosis: **Suffered from hallucinations and disorientation**

Mickey Featherstone was born into a large, poor Irish family on New York City's West Side, in a tough, working-class neighborhood known as Hell's Kitchen. He was one of nine children. His mother did some work—though much of it was volunteer work—for the Veterans of Foreign Wars. His father did the best he could to provide for the family by working as a custom's officer at the nearby port.

As a child and teenager, Featherstone had blond hair and a baby face—looks that belied his violent temper and fearless nature. When he was only seventeen, he lied about his age in order to be admitted to the US Army's Green Beret division, so that he could go fight in the Vietnam War.

Even before enlisting, Featherstone had shown himself to be reckless and sometimes out of control. His family welcomed the discipline the army might be able to instill in him. But after serving a year in Vietnam as a clerk and never seeing combat, Featherstone started having hallucinations. He was discharged from the army and sent back to his old neighborhood, where an Irish gang known as The Westies controlled things.

Francis Featherstone is taken into custody at Forest Hills Police Station in New York.

He was in and out of mental hospitals for the next eight years. When he was not hospitalized, he was killing people—sometimes for The Westies and sometimes because someone insulted him. For example, in 1971 he shot and killed a man outside a bar because the man had insulted him. Police found him several hours later, still clutching his gun and mumbling incoherently. He was found not guilty by reason of insanity. That decision to let him go resulted in many more murders.

Out of control and known as a wild man, Featherstone was just what James Coonan needed. Coonan was a rising Irish gangster who had his eyes on taking over The Westies, but he didn't have the muscle to make a move like that. In 1976, Coonan enlisted

Featherstone to help him murder the leader, Mickey Spillane. Featherstone was arrested for Spillane's murder but was acquitted.

It was also during this time that The Westies, now Coonan's gang, started taking on contract work from the Gambino crime family in the Italian Mafia. The man to do many of the killings was,, of course, Featherstone. He would sometimes cut the hands off of some of his victims and keep them in his freezer. This would allow him to plant fingerprints at other crimes he committed and keep the police from thinking anyone had been murdered.

But his behavior became more erratic. He was not disposing of bodies in the proper way the Mafia had instructed, and some of his handiwork was being discovered by police. He also had a falling out with Coonan over his relationship with the Italians.

After being arrested for a 1986 murder, Featherstone turned state's witness against Coonan and went into witness protection, meaning he would testify against his friend and tell the police everything they had done.

Danger signs:

Unstable, hallucinations

Pattern of attack:

Various methods

Number of victims:

Believed to be a dozen

Richard Leonard Kuklinski

aka Iceman

Born: **April 11, 1935**

Occupation: **Professional hitman**

Diagnosis: **Antisocial and paranoid personality disorder; bipolar disorder**

Died: **May 5, 2006 in prison**

Richard Kuklinski has been classified as a serial killer, spree killer, and hitman. All three labels fit perfectly. Kuklinski was actually born in his family's New Jersey apartment to a Polish immigrant father and Irish-American mother. They were very harsh parents, and his childhood was nothing short of a nightmare. They both severely beat him and his two brothers.

His parents beat Kuklinski's older brother so badly that he died from his injuries. The family lied to police and said the boy had fallen down the stairs. It was not long after that Kuklinski began displaying the dangerous trait of hurting animals when he started killing neighborhood cats.

By the time he was twenty, Kuklinski had earned the reputation of being a pool shark in New Jersey, who would often beat or even kill those who insulted him. His younger brother was convicted of raping and killing a twelve-year-old girl. He was sentenced to life in prison.

Kuklinski's fearless attitude and toughness attracted the attention of the local Italian Mafia family, and they started contracting him to perform murders for them. But Kuklinski was not content with those murder-for-hire deals. He would tell investigators much later in his life that during that time he would drive from New Jersey across the Hudson River to New York's West Side and would just find random people to kill. It was there, killing vagrants, homeless people, or basically anyone that looked at him the wrong way that Kuklinski mastered how to kill and properly dispose of bodies. He worked by a certain code, however, refusing to kill women or children.

A doctor at Trenton State Prison years later said that Kuklinski inherited antisocial behavior from his parents, but he was also greatly affected by his violent and harsh upbringing, combining both nature and nurture theories for the factors affecting an individual's behavior.

In order to earn complete trust of the Mafia, Kuklinski was ordered to kill a random person—at their choosing. They selected a man walking his dog one night. Without hesitation, Kuklinski exited the car, walked over to the man, and shot him in the back of the head.

Kuklinski committed dozens of murders, perhaps even hundreds, during the next decade. As he got older however, he started experimenting with different methods, and his actions almost made it seem as if he wanted to get caught. He earned the nickname "Iceman," not only from his cool demeanor but because he started freezing victims in order to disguise the exact time of their deaths.

He once killed a man, put his body in a closed barrel, and left it outside a busy diner. Then he returned to the diner every day

Richard "The Iceman" Kuklinski stands in a courtroom in this scene from
the 2001 documentary *The Iceman Confesses: Secrets of a Mafia Hitman*.

to see if it would be discovered. It never was. He practiced killing techniques on innocent strangers using poison and once even firing a bolt from a crossbow into a stranger's head.

He was finally arrested after agreeing to kill someone for a mobster, who turned out to be a police informant. He died in prison but only after agreeing to numerous interviews and medical and mental health examinations.

Danger signs:

Bad temper, need for revenge

Pattern of attack:

Used all types; started by killing those who insulted him

Number of victims:

Convicted of killing five people; believed to have killed at least one hundred

aka Sammy "The Bull" Gravano

Born: March 12, 1945

Occupation: Underboss for the Gambino crime family

Diagnosis: None

Before Salvatore "Sammy the Bull" Gravano became known as the biggest Mafia "rat" ever, he had the reputation of being one of its most feared and cold-blooded killers.

When members are sworn into the Mafia, they take the oath of Omerta, which states that no member can ever give evidence to the police about their illegal activities. When Gravano testified against mob boss John Gotti, he became the highest-ranking mobster ever to turn state's witness.

Gravano was born in Brooklyn and was the youngest of three children and the only boy in the family. From a young age, his family thought he looked like his uncle Sammy and started calling him by that name. He was always tough and no stranger to trouble growing up. He was caught stealing cupcakes and once singlehandedly beat up a group that had stolen his bicycle. That earned him the nickname Bull.

After a stint in the US Army, Gravano returned home and worked with his father for a while. They would often pass a tavern where known Mafia members hung out, and despite his father pleading with his son not to join, Gravano was pulled in by the lifestyle and soon became part of the Colombo crime family.

Making money as a loan shark and thief, Gravano committed his first murder in 1971, killing a man who was plotting to kill him. The murder earned him great respect within the family.

Interestingly enough, after Gravano joined the Gambino family, he started working in construction and wanted to leave the life of crime behind. But after being accused of a murder he did not commit, Gravano needed money to hire an attorney. In his book *Underboss*, Gravano said he went on an eighteen-month robbery spree in order to pay for a lawyer and never looked back. After beating the murder rap, he was an entrenched mobster.

Gravano's next murder was that of his wife's brother, who had insulted a Mafia boss. Only the man's hands were found and no one ever learned how he was killed. Then Gravano—who was on crutches at the time—killed the leader of a motorcycle gang that had trashed his club.

Gravano became involved with construction racketeering and became a millionaire. He opened a successful night club and agreed

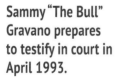

Sammy "The Bull" Gravano prepares to testify in court in April 1993.

to sell it to an investor. But when the new owner insulted him, Gravano killed him.

He performed several more murders for his boss, Paul Castellano, who had a rule about his men not dealing drugs. When several men were indicted for drug trafficking, Gravano and rising mob boss John Gotti conspired to kill Castellano as he exited a steak house in midtown New York City.

He killed and ordered the murders of many others under Gotti's reign. But after being arrested and charged with murder, Gravano decided to save his own skin and testify against Gotti. His testimony sent Gotti and numerous other mobsters to prison for life.

Despite having killed nineteen people, Gravano was sentenced to only five years in prison for his help and then was placed in the witness protection program. He later left the program and was arrested on drug charges.

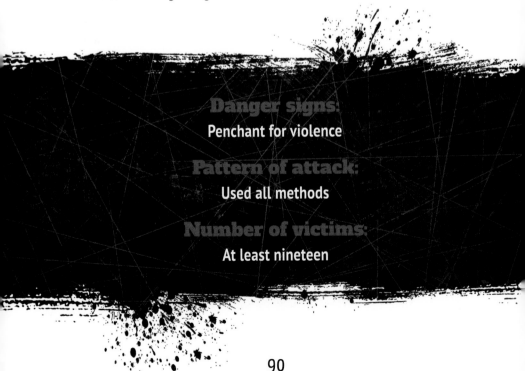

Danger signs:

Penchant for violence

Pattern of attack:

Used all methods

Number of victims:

At least nineteen

Salvatore Riina
aka Salvatore "The Beast" Riina

Born: November 16, 1930
Occupation: Chief of the Sicilian Mafia
Diagnosis: Sociopath, narcissist

Salvatore Riina was born in a very poor home, to a poverty-stricken family in the small countryside town of Corleone, Italy. Coincidentally, this is the same Sicilian town where the fictional character Vito Corleone is from in the *Godfather* movies. Something happened when Riina was a teen that certainly shaped his future in a negative way.

Because the family was so poor, when his father found an unexploded American bomb in the countryside, he planned to open the bomb and sell its parts, including the gunpowder. But he did not know what he was doing and the bomb exploded, killing him and one of his children—Salvatore Riina's seven-year-old brother.

That incident made the young Riina—a teenager at the time—the male head of the family. In order to provide for his mother and siblings, he joined the local Mafia gang when he was only nineteen years old. This was made possible because his uncle was already a member. Riina's initiation involved murdering someone to prove his loyalty. The following year he killed someone else during an argument and served time in prison.

When he got out, the hardened and vicious Riina became one of the family's most prolific enforcers, murdering just about everyone from the previous regime as well as anyone who went against his

Corleone is a small town in Sicily, Italy. It is the birthplace of Mafia boss Salvatore Riina and his faction.

family's mob activities. He also earned money by extorting business owners and stealing livestock.

He rose to power in 1974 and became the head of the family, which had ambitions to take over the heroin trade from its rival families. Instead of negotiating, Riina embarked on a reign of terror in which he started a war with the other families, and ordered the murder of judges, police, prosecutors, and politicians. Eventually Riina took over the heroin trade.

His brutality and murderous tendencies knew little boundary. In 1984, while his family was under major investigation for its criminal activities, Riina masterminded and ordered a train to be bombed in order to distract the authorities from investigating him further.

Salvatore Riina is seen behind bars during a trial in Rome on April 29, 1993.

The People Behind Murderous Crime Sprees

The December 23, 1984, attack became known as the Christmas massacre, which killed seventeen people and wounded nearly three hundred. Riina's plan worked to perfection. Terrorists were blamed, and the government was no longer intent on indicting him. It was later learned that he also considered plans to bomb and destroy several famous Italian landmarks and tourist destinations, including the Tower of Pisa.

Years later, when he was finally tracked down and arrested, newspapers printed photographs of him calling him The Devil. When it was all said and done, Riina was accused of personally murdering forty people and ordering hundreds more murdered. Riina's two sons followed their father into the family business and have spent time in prison for various crimes committed.

Riina was sentenced to life in prison in Italy, the harshest sentence allowed in that country.

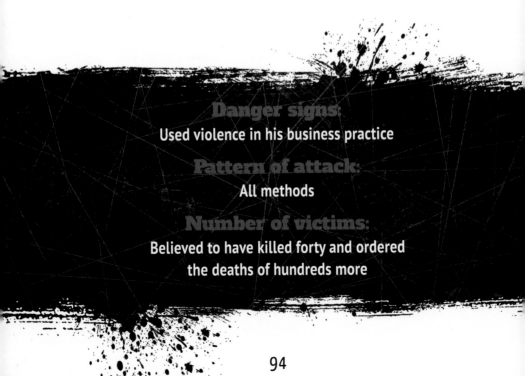

Danger signs:

Used violence in his business practice

Pattern of attack:

All methods

Number of victims:

Believed to have killed forty and ordered
the deaths of hundreds more

Giovanni Brusca

aka Giovanni "The Pig" Brusca

Born: **February 20, 1957**

Occupation: **Mob boss**

Diagnosis: **Sociopath**

Ruthless killer Giovanni Brusca was born in Sicily, Italy, in 1957. The "nature versus nurture" debate doesn't apply in his case. Brusca never really had a chance to be anything but a violent criminal and murderer. His grandfather and great-grandfather were well-known Mafia members, and his father was the local Mafia boss. Once he was old enough, it was expected that Brusca follow the family tradition of crime. His two brothers—one younger and one older—also joined the Mafia.

Brusca was known to have a violent temper as a child and exhibited a fearless attitude, likely brought about by the fact that no one would ever hurt him because of his family's status in the Mafia. By the time he was twenty years old, Brusca—nicknamed The Pig for his unkempt manner—was driving for one of the top bosses. Within a few years, he became part of Salvatore Riina's death squad, where he carried out numerous murders on the orders of the family. He was known for being relentless in his desire to eliminate his enemies and those who even opposed him during his rise to the top.

But none of Brusca's murders can compare to one particular atrocity that shocked even the most hardened mob members and broke a code that had long stood regarding the killing of women

Giovanni Brusca was one of Italy's most wanted fugitives. He is escorted by masked policemen outside police headquarters in Palermo, Sicily, in 1996.

and children. After Santo Di Matteo was arrested for murder, he decided to cooperate with police, going against the Mafia code. Brusca's response? He ordered men to pose as police and kidnap Di Matteo's eleven-year-old son. He held him for more than two years, torturing and punishing the boy. They sent photos of his torture to the boy's father to get him to recant his testimony. Eventually the boy was strangled and his body placed in a vat of acid so his family could not even perform a funeral. That was deemed as another taboo broken by Brusca.

Brusca's ruthless nature was also evident when he responded to a government crackdown on mob-related activities by planting a series of bombs around densely populated tourist spots. The bombs killed ten innocent bystanders and injured over seventy people.

When special prosecutor Giovanni Falcone refused to back off, he became the target of Brusca's rage. The Pig eventually killed Falcone and his wife along with several bodyguards, when he detonated a bomb in a car they were traveling in. Brusca himself is believed to have pressed the button igniting the bomb.

When he was arrested by authorities in 1996, Brusca shocked the mob world and his own father, who was serving life in prison by cooperating with police in exchange for leniency. His confessions and allegations were shocking, including one that the country's prime minister, Silvio Berlusconi, had cooperated and even paid the Mafia to keep things orderly in the country. The government was harshly criticized for showing leniency to such a violent man and child murderer.

Brusca once testified that he killed between 100 and 200 people but did not know the exact number.

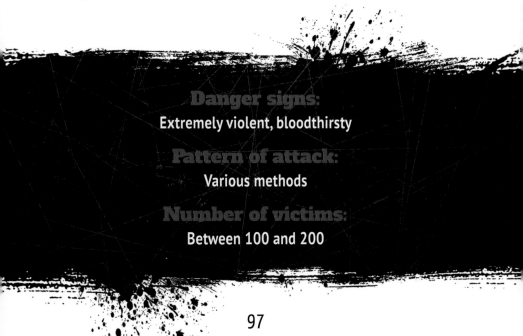

Danger signs:

Extremely violent, bloodthirsty

Pattern of attack:

Various methods

Number of victims:

Between 100 and 200

Chapter 5

Drug-Fueled

MURDER SPREES

Illegal drugs and drug abuse has been referred to as the scourge of society. And it's true. Some of the byproduct of the drug trade includes addiction, violence, poverty, hopelessness, and more crime. Drug addicts stealing money to buy more drugs, drug lords and cartels ordering the assassination of their rivals, and street corner drug dealers killing someone who has moved into their territory are all examples of how the drug trade often leads to violence. Sometimes the violence is committed by those selling, sometimes by those buying, and sometimes by those using.

Of course, the driving factors behind the illegal drug trade go far beyond simple right and wrong. There is no greater factor than socioeconomic reasons. For example, the tiny country of El Salvador

Drug dealing, supplying, and abuse can all lead people into a life that involves shootings and killings.

is home to forty thousand violent gang members. And it is no accident that drug use and open drug dealing is more prevalent in poverty-stricken neighborhoods in the United States.

A case in point is the story of Florida felon Wade Dante Jackson, someone who you will never hear about but who is serving out a twenty-year prison sentence. Jackson, who was raised by a single mother in a poor, high-crime area of Brevard County, was only eighteen years old when he was wrongfully arrested and charged with murder. He spent more than a full year in jail awaiting trial, when he was cleared by DNA testing and released. His missed his grandfather's passing and funeral while locked up.

Unable to find a job, he turned to selling drugs on the corner. His mother didn't like it but she said he was out of choices. He needed to earn money on his own. Eventually Dante was arrested several more times on drug charges, and a weapons charge sent him away for twenty years.[1]

Criminologists have come up with several theories, including the social disorganization theory, strain theory, and the cultural deviance theory, to help explain and understand the rate of crime in poorer, socially dysfunctional neighborhoods. The theories examine the effects of family, businesses, and schools on a neighborhood and whether the system is broken down. They also look at the frustrations that some of the residents in these poorer areas face when trying to break out of their socioeconomic class.

Criminologists understand the problems caused by poverty and income inequality. Varied sources of crime data show that crime rates are highest in neighborhoods with poverty and social disorder.[2]

In addition to the socioeconomic factors that can influence a person's mental health, there are also biological factors that play a major part. Although the impact of poverty and peers on drug use is often emphasized, biological influences also affect drug use. In order to understand the biology of substance use, one must appreciate not only the effect of each substance on biology, but also the effect of an individual's biology on his or her potential to abuse drugs.[3]

This chapter looks at some of the extreme cases of drug violence; it may surprise the reader that not all the cases involve inner-city, poverty-stricken neighborhoods. One involves a murderous cult leader, while another involves one of the world's most infamous drug lords.

Dale Merle Nelson

Born: March 19, 1939

Occupation: Logger

Diagnosis: Depression; alcohol and drug abuse

Died: In 1999 from cancer while in prison

Dale Nelson liked to party. The problem was he could never quite control his drinking or his extensive drug use. And when he did go on a bender, the Canadian would oftentimes get violent.

Not much has been noted about the man's childhood. He was born in British Columbia and his father was apparently a big drinker as well. Nelson loved the hallucinogenic drug LSD and enjoyed the mind-bending effects.

Nelson did, however, function well enough in order to find a wife and raise three children, while he worked outdoors as a logger. He enjoyed the outdoors and was an avid hunter and fisherman. For a while the family enjoyed a happy, peaceful life. But the drug abuse worsened and with that, he became sexually dysfunctional. The violence increased when he could not perform sexually.

Some reports say that he physically abused his wife and sexually abused his children in order to prove to himself that he could perform. It was during that time period—in 1970—that Nelson tried unsuccessfully to kill himself. The attempt and his depressed state caused him to be placed in a mental hospital for the next two months.

Dale Nelson's murder spree took place in Creston, British Columbia, Canada.

When he emerged, friends say he started behaving even more erratically; and everything changed on a night in September 1970 in Creston, British Columbia. On a bender fueled by alcohol and drugs, Nelson went on a killing spree that included mutilation and reports of cannibalism and necrophilia.

He started the night of mayhem just after midnight, when he went to the home of his cousin Shirley Wasyk and beat her to death with a fire extinguisher. He then went after her three daughters, one at a time, forcing the youngest to perform a sexual act on him. He killed another of the daughters with a large hunting knife. He took the body with him as he ventured out to the home of a family he did not know. There, he shot and killed four more people—including an eighteen-month-old boy. Nelson took an eight-year-old girl from the home and went on the run.

Police started an immediate manhunt, even using planes to help spot Nelson's pickup truck. They also evacuated the remaining 150 residents of the small town to ensure their safety.

After Nelson's truck was spotted by a plane and police moved in, he started cutting up the body of the girl he had killed earlier. He left body parts scattered in the area. Police officers followed the grisly trail of dismembered pieces to a sleeping Nelson. Beside him was the bound and gagged body of the kidnapped eight-year-old. She was dead, killed by a knife in her back.

Nelson was found guilty and was sentenced to life in prison.

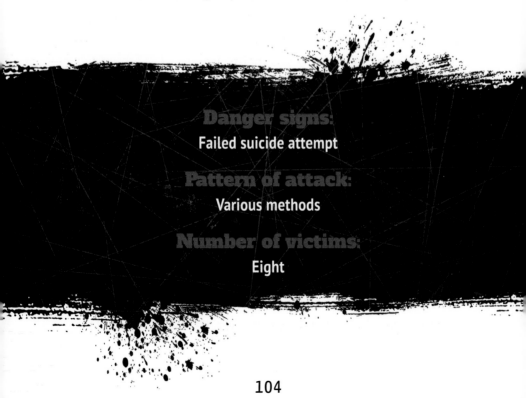

Danger signs:

Failed suicide attempt

Pattern of attack:

Various methods

Number of victims:

Eight

Archibald Beattie McCafferty

Born: **1948**

Occupation: **Sanitation worker**

Diagnosis: **Delusions; paranoid schizophrenia**

T he future seemed bright for the McCafferty family. They left behind a bleak, working-class existence in Scotland to follow their dreams in Australia. An only child, Archibald McCafferty was constantly getting into trouble at school and with police, even as a young child. He was so uncontrollable that he was locked up in a home for juvenile delinquents when he was only twelve years old.

Authorities and child psychologists ignored obvious warning signs, including McCafferty's admissions that he enjoyed torturing and killing small animals, including chickens, cats, and dogs. The reason was because none of his crimes up until that point had been violent in nature. By the time he was eighteen, McCafferty had already been locked up five times for a variety of petty crimes.

It turns out that adulthood did not help make him a better criminal. He amassed thirty-five convictions by the age of twenty-four, for all sorts of infractions including theft, burglary, larceny, assault, and dealing in stolen goods.

In 1972, McCafferty married his pregnant girlfriend, Janice Redington, but nearly killed her when she found him in bed with another woman only a few weeks later. He was admitted to a

Archibald Beattie McCafferty was locked up as a juvenile delinquent. He later killed four people.

psychiatric hospital, but upon his release he began drinking heavily and self-medicating with illegal drugs.

This began a continual pattern of physically abusing his wife and then checking himself into a mental hospital. He was always able to check himself out because he went in voluntarily. But the drinking and drug abuse became worse with each visit. He even told a doctor in the mental hospital that he wanted to kill his wife and her family.

Things did not get much better after his son was born, as the violent outbursts and violent behavior continued. But things changed drastically the night of a terrible accident that claimed his young son's life. His mother had taken the baby into their bed in order to breastfeed him in the middle of the night, when she fell asleep and rolled over on the child and suffocated him.

The police cleared the young mother, calling it an accident. But McCafferty never forgave her. He left her and called her a murderer. He checked himself into the state hospital again but was never quite the same. Months went by, and he continued to threaten his former wife and her family with death.

As he delved deeper into mental instability, McCafferty somehow convinced a band of teenagers and ne'er-do-wells to follow him down a violent path. One night, while carousing and looking for an easy mark to rob, they attacked a fifty-year-old man, and McCafferty beat him and stabbed him to death. McCafferty had been smoking angel dust all night.

After the murder he started hearing his son's voice in his head, telling him that he would be reborn if McCafferty killed seven people. He killed his second victim a few nights later, near his son's grave, then ordered his followers to shoot and kill someone they kidnapped a few hours later.

His plan was to make his wife his final victim and sever her head. But police caught him after three murders, and he was sentenced to life in prison, where he killed another inmate, bringing the number to four. Years later, McCafferty convinced psychologists he was better, and Australian authorities deported him to Scotland, where he lives as a free man.

Danger signs:

Killed animals as a child; started hearing voices

Pattern of attack:

Random

Number of victims:

Four but wanted to kill seven

Joaquín Archivaldo Guzmán Loera

Aka Joaquin "El Chapo" Guzman

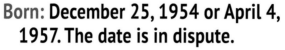

> **Born:** December 25, 1954 or April 4, 1957. The date is in dispute.
>
> **Occupation:** Drug lord and boss of massive Mexican criminal enterprise
>
> **Diagnosis:** Psychopath

Well before Joaquin "El Chapo" Guzmán made international headlines in 2015 by brazenly escaping from a Mexican prison via tunnel and underground motorized train car, he had established himself as one of the world's most notorious killers. He is regularly listed as one of the world's most powerful men and is listed as one of the richest men in the world as well. He is sometimes compared to infamous American gangster Al Capone in notoriety.

Guzmán was born in the small, rural farming town of El Tuna, Mexico. This is where generation after generation of his family had lived and tilled the soil or raised livestock. Guzmán's father was a cattle rancher, who is believed to have also grown poppy plants for opium production. Like other farmers in the area, his father also cultivated marijuana. Guzmán was nicknamed Chapo, which means *shorty*, and as a child he would try to help the family by selling oranges.

He quit school by the third grade in order to help his father with the business, and by the age of fifteen he was running his own marijuana farm. Without much hope of ever breaking out of his socioeconomic class, Guzmán asked an uncle to help him enter the world of organized crime.

He impressed his new bosses almost immediately with his ferocious and volatile nature. Put in charge of a drug delivery supply line, Guzmán did not hesitate to simply put a bullet in the head of someone he deemed to be careless, unreliable, or untrustworthy. He killed hundreds and rose quickly through the ranks, expanding his business to include not only marijuana but cocaine and methamphetamine as well. He was arrested in 1993 and sentenced to twenty years in prison before spending $2.5 million in bribes to escape a few years later. It was his first escape from prison.

As Guzmán's position grew stronger and alliances were made with cartels in other countries, his atrocities increased as well. Guzmán had no trouble executing hundreds of soldiers and sending their heads as warnings to anyone who might try to bring him down. It is not uncommon for Guzmán to include a note with a decapitated head, openly threatening someone. In 2011 he had five headless bodies placed near an elementary school with a note threatening teachers to pay half of their salaries to him for "protection."

But even worse is his war on religion—namely Christianity, which is prominent in Mexico. He has ordered the executions of priests who speak out against what he does and against missionaries and other religious people.

He was arrested in 2014 after a joint operation between Mexican and US authorities, and after many of his top men had been captured or killed. By mid-July 2015 he had escaped and was once again loose to continue his killing sprees.

RECOMPENSA
60 MILLONES DE PESOS

La Procuraduría General de la República ofrece una recompensa de 60 millones de pesos a quien proporcione información confiable que lleve a la captura del delincuente Joaquín Guzmán Loera, alias "El Chapo", condenado a prisión.

Llama al
088

A notice was published in newspapers offering a reward to anyone with information leading to the recapture of Joaquin "El Chapo" Guzman in Mexico City on July 16, 2015.

While on the run, he agreed to be interviewed by American movie star and social activist Sean Penn for *Rolling Stone* magazine. Penn was criticized for posing for photographs with the killer.

The authorities apprehended Guzmán in Mexico after a shootout and he is back behind bars—for now.

Danger signs:

Ruthless killer

Pattern of attack:

Random

Number of victims:

He claims to have had 2,000 to 3,000 people killed.

Margie Velma Barfield

Born: **October 29, 1932**

Occupation: **Housewife and caretaker for the elderly**

Diagnosis: **Addiction**

Died: **November 2, 1984, execution**

Velma Barfield is unique in that she is a female and is considered by many to be a serial killer. Her addiction to drugs complicates matters even more, as most serial killers choose their victims carefully and oftentimes have no connection to their victims.

Barfield's path to murderess began during her childhood in Fayetteville, North Carolina. Her father was a failed tobacco farmer and strict disciplinarian. He would often beat his nine children, including the second oldest—Velma. She resented the beatings and especially resented how her mother did little to protect her from her violent father.

As a young student, she posted good grades but started stealing in order to have better clothes to wear to school. Though she was popular—in part because she was a good basketball player—she felt the kids would never accept her because she was so poor.

She married as soon as she was legally able, to seventeen-year-old Thomas Burke. The two seemed to enjoy a happy life and were content raising their two children. But Velma's life and future path was altered when she had a hysterectomy. The operation carried with it complications that could only be alleviated by pain pills and valium.

Velma Barfield, shown here during an interview in 1984, was convicted in 1978 of poisoning several members of her family.

Velma killed her husband and disguised it as a house fire in order to collect an insurance check. A few years later, a second husband died as well. After her father passed away from lung cancer, Velma went to go live with her mother, who started experiencing stomach pains. By Christmas her mother was dead.

Velma soon took on a job caring for the elderly in their homes. But her next three clients soon died as well. Finally, while attending a Christian revival featuring a famous preacher, her latest love interest—a live-in boyfriend—collapsed, complaining of severe stomach cramping. He was dead before the police could arrive. A call made by one of Velma's suspicious relatives alerted police to the possibility of poison, which was later confirmed.

When she later confessed to the murders, she would tell police that the reason she did it was to conceal from her victims the fact that she had been stealing a lot of money from them in order to support her drug addiction. Her lawyers argued unsuccessfully in court that she should be charged only with second-degree murder because her intent was to make her victims ill and not actually kill them. A jury did not believe it.

She was sentenced to death and became a born-again Christian while on death row; she was executed despite a public outcry to spare her life. During her final statement made moments before being executed, she apologized to all those she hurt.

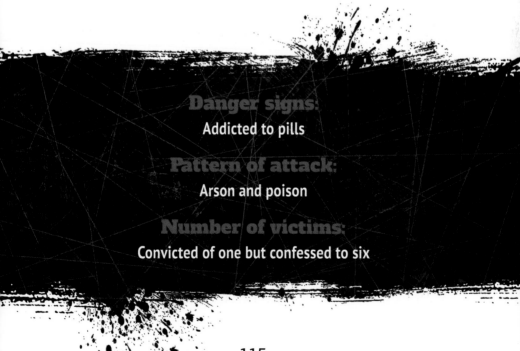

Danger signs:

Addicted to pills

Pattern of attack:

Arson and poison

Number of victims:

Convicted of one but confessed to six

Born: May 13, 1931

Occupation: Preacher, cult leader

Diagnosis: Messiah complex, paranoia, and drug addiction

Died: November 18, 1978

Jim Jones was regarded by many as the worst mass murderer of all time when he convinced hundreds of his followers to drink poison. But a spree killer? Since he killed on more than one occasion and within a short span of time, he can also fit the description of a spree killer.

Jones was born in a small rural town in Indiana. And if he suffered from a messiah complex from a very young age, the blame can go to his mother. She was under the delusion that she was giving birth to the messiah.

As a child, Jones loved to read, but he became obsessed with the writings of some of the world's most brutal and murderous dictators, like Josef Stalin and Adolph Hitler. He wanted to learn their weaknesses. He was also very interested in religion and death, which made for a lonely childhood, as most kids his age considered him weird.

His father was a racist and a reported member of the Ku Klux Klan. The two reportedly did not speak for many years because of their views regarding race. Jones got married in 1949 and went to college at night, earning a degree in secondary education. But

Dead bodies lie around the compound of the People's Temple cult on November 18, 1978, after the more than nine hundred members of the cult, led by Reverend Jim Jones, died from drinking cyanide-laced Kool-Aid. They were victims of the largest mass suicide in modern history.

during that time he also became a pastor in a Christian church, where he became ingrained in the civil rights movement for African Americans. He also traveled a lot to other countries, where he studied local religious beliefs.

In the early 1970s, he was arrested for soliciting a man for sex and was believed to be bisexual, though he said he hated homosexual activities.

As the years went on, his teachings and his close-knit congregation came under scrutiny for being a socialist cult that did not allow members to leave, and where Jones would sexually abuse the members.

To avoid more attention, he moved the church to Guyana in Central America and started a community called Jonestown. Over time, some members escaped, but others could not. This caused relatives and friends in the United States to become concerned and pressure politicians to intervene.

US Congressman Leo Ryan paid a visit to Jonestown; along with some concerned family members, wanting to see if their relatives were being held against their will. Ryan toured the grounds and was about to board a plane back to the states when Jones ordered his men to open fire on the group, killing Ryan and four others. A few hours later, Jones instructed his congregation—over nine hundred people, including his wife—to ingest a cyanide-laced drink. Jones, who convinced his followers that the end was near and that his paranoia regarding intelligence agents conspiring against them was real, ordered followers to poison their children first before ingesting the cyanide themselves. More than three hundred of the victims were children.

Jones then shot himself in the head.

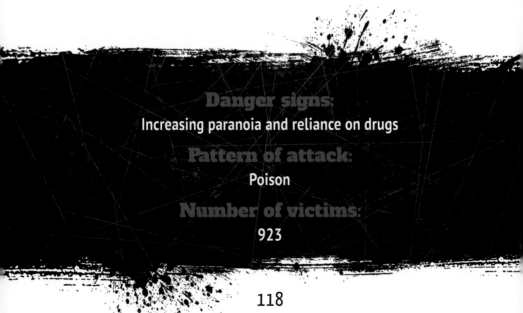

Danger signs:
Increasing paranoia and reliance on drugs

Pattern of attack:
Poison

Number of victims:
923

CONCLUSION

Whether they fit neatly into one specific killer category or not, the people profiled in this book offer a serious challenge to criminologists, psychologists, and anyone trying to understand why. While many of the killers suffered through horrendous childhoods or experienced traumatic events, that does not begin to explain why everyone who has experienced a rough upbringing or suffered heartbreaking events at a young age does not go on to become a murderer.

That's where the nature-versus-nurture theory comes into play as a main factor. How much of what shapes a person's behavior is genetics and how much is the result of bad parenting? But then one must also account for substance abuse issues, socioeconomic issues, and other extraneous factors.

One of the problems facing researchers is the lack of reliable data. For example, there exists only one study—conducted by the University of Massachusetts—that includes extensive data and interviews with violent felons incarcerated in several prisons in ten states. Law enforcement officials still rely on the study, despite it being done in 1985. The study includes important data regarding escalating violence, drug use, mental illness, and other personal information.

Today, privacy laws—especially when it pertains to medical information—can hinder the research needed to understand the motivations behind a potential killer and perhaps do something to stop it.

It is too often the case in many of these high-profile or especially gruesome murders that the victims are forgotten. The fascination tends to gravitate toward the killer. How could they do it? Why did they do it? Why was there no one there to stop them?

We can name Bonnie and Clyde, Charles Starkweather, and John Gotti but can we name one of their victims? We cannot allow them to be forgotten or else we risk becoming desensitized ourselves.

Let's also remember to give credit to the numerous professionals in the law enforcement and mental health fields that work tirelessly to understand and ultimately help those prone to violence, in part due to addiction or mental illness.

Chapter Notes

Introduction

1. Mark Roth, "Experts Track the Patterns of Mass Murders," *Pittsburgh Post-Gazette*, April 13, 2009, http://www.post-gazette.com/local/city /2009/04/13/Experts-track-the-patterns-of-mass-murders/stories /200904130098 (accessed March 2, 2016).
2. Ronald M. Holmes and Stephen T. Holmes, *Profiling Violent Crimes: An Investigative Tool* (Thousand Oaks, CA: Sage Publications, 2009), p. 58.
3. Robert J. Morton, ed. The Federal Bureau of Investigation. *Serial Murder: Multi-Disciplinary Reports for Investigators.* https://www.fbi.gov/stats-services /publications/serial-murder (accessed Feb. 7, 2016).

Chapter 1: Duos

1. Larry J. Siegel, *Criminology,* 10th ed. (Lowell, MA: University of Massachusetts Press, 2009), p. 98.
2. *The Encyclopedia of Murderers,* "Charles Raymond Starkweather." http:// murderpedia.org/male.S/s/starkweather.htm (accessed Dec. 10, 2015).
3. Colander, Pat, "True Crime: The Murder Spree of Alton Coleman and Debra Brown," *The Times of Northwest Indiana*, July 30, 2015, <http://www.nwitimes .com/news/state-and-regional/true-crime-the-murder-spree-of-alton -coleman-and-debra/article_05b1a602-dd94-5e53-8f4e-345681725c4d .htm. (accessed Dec. 10, 2015).
4. Mark Gribben, "Alton Coleman and Debra Brown: The Odyssey of Mayhem, <http://www.murderpedia.org/male.C/c1/coleman-alton.htm> (accessed Dec. 10, 2015).

Chapter 2: Solo Killers

1. Larry J. Siegel, *Criminology,* 10th ed. (Lowell, MA: University of Massachusetts Press, 2009), p. 24.
2. Ronald M. Holmes and Stephen T. Holmes, *Profiling Violent Crimes: An Investigative Tool* (Thousand Oaks, CA: Sage Publications, 2009), p. 66.
3. Ibid., p. 2.
4. Donald W. Black and C. Linden Larsen, "Bad Boys, Bad Men: Confronting Anti-Social Personality Disorder," (New York: Oxford University Press, 1999), p. 7.

Chapter 3: Rampage Killers

1. Larry J. Siegel, *Criminology*, 10th ed. (Lowell, MA: University of Massachusetts Press, 2009), p. 300.
2. PBS, "Mind of a Rampage Killer," *NOVA*, February 20, 2013.
3. John A. Torres, "Killer on Death Row Two Decades After Massacre," *Florida Today*, April 23, 2007, p. 1A.
4. Kevin Sack, "Shootings in Atlanta: The Overview," *New York Times*, July 31, 1999, <http://www.nytimes.com/1999/07/31/us/shootings-in-atlanta-the-overview-killer-confessed-in-a-letter-spiked-with-rage.html?pagewanted=all> (accessed, Dec. 22, 2015).

Chapter 5: Drug-Fueled Murder Sprees

1. Torres, John A., "Cleared of Murder, Jackson Still Gets 20 Years," *Florida Today Newspaper*, Oct. 8, 2015, p. 3A.
2. Larry J. Siegel, *Criminology*, 10th ed. (Lowell, MA: University of Massachusetts Press, 2009), p. 166.
3. Charles C. Beidel, Cynthia M Bulik, and Melinda A. Stanley, *Abnormal Psychology* (Saddle River NJ: Prentice Hall Publishers, 2010), p. 315.

Glossary

attributes–A certain quality of someone's personality.

ballistic–Relating to projectiles and their flight.

bootleggers–Those who make and sell items illegally.

carnage–A slaughter or killing of lots of people.

categorize–To put something into a certain grouping or category.

deviance–Doing something outside the usual accepted social boundaries.

dismember–To cut off the arms and legs of a person or animal.

dyslexia–A disorder affecting someone's reading ability.

genocide–The execution or murder of a large group of people belonging to one ethnic or religious group.

heinous–Something evil or wicked.

icon–A person highly regarded as a symbol for a movement or group.

incompetency–Not able to perform at acceptable levels.

inherited–To receive a personality trait from a parent or ancestor.

mechanism–An accepted way of doing things; a process.

notorious–Famous for doing something bad.

retribution–A punishment for doing something bad.

revival–An improvement to make something new again.

tendency–What someone is more inclined or likely to do.

Further Reading

Books

Hickey, Eric. *Serial Killers and Their Victims*. Belmont, CA: Wadsworth Publishing, 2012.

Latta, Sara. *Medical Serial Killers*. New York: Enslow Publishing, 2016.

Rauf, Don. *Female Serial Killers*. New York: Enslow Publishing, 2016.

Woog, Adam. *Careers in the FBI*. New York: Cavendish Square, 2014.

Websites

The Federal Bureau of Investigation
fbi.gov/stats-services/publications
Reports and publications regarding the study of violent criminals, including serial, spree, and rampage killers.

Murderpedia.org
murderpedia.org/
This encyclopedia contains biographies of murderers, listed alphabetically.

Psychology Today
psychologytoday.com/blog/wicked-deeds/201407/ why-spree-killers-are-not-serial-killers
Read about the difference between spree killers and serial killers.

Index

126